topical punch

topical punch

Saucy Songs by
Nancy White

METHUEN

TORONTO NEW YORK LONDON SYDNEY AUCKLAND

Canadian Cataloguing in Publication Data

White, Nancy.
  Topical punch

Discography: p.
Includes index.
ISBN 0-458-80200-X

1. Satirical songs — Canada.   2. Songs, English —
Canada.   3. Satirical songs — Canada — Texts.
4. Songs, English — Canada — Texts.   I. Title.

M1977.H7W58 1986   784.6'8   C86-093348-2

DESIGN: William Fox/Associates
COVER PHOTO: Plum Studios Incorporated

Printed and bound in Canada

1 2 3 4   86   90 89 88 87

Contents

topical punch

Introduction

The legend goes in my family that I became a singer because my mother was frightened by Ethel Merman while she was carrying me.

I do know that I became a songwriter so that I could have material in my own range and key. (Sheet music is almost always written in men's keys – makes me crazy!)

I started writing novelty songs in college because I wanted to sing on the stage but thought my voice was pretty ordinary and if I wanted to get people's attention, I should try to make them laugh.

I started writing songs about the news when someone offered me money to do it. The someone was Mark Starowicz, who in the fall of 1976 was starting a CBC public affairs radio show called "Sunday Morning" and figured it would need some light stuff.

He was right about that and I was thrilled at being hired to work on the show. I stayed for two and a half years, writing at least three topical songs a week and recording them with a lot of help from the producers – first Sharon Keogh, then the legendary Ivan Fecan.

There were some great perks. I won an ACTRA award, recorded an album, made Ugandan Peanut Butter Stew on "Celebrity Cooks," became a household word in Canada's stranger households, and of course had access to the photocopy machine – but eventually I burned out and quit in the spring of '79. I had written probably 500 songs and figured that was plenty.

Besides, people were starting to see me as this political pundit, whereas I saw myself as a singer even though I had no drug problems and didn't like playing clubs very much.

Two years after I'd left the show, people were still assuring me that they listened to me every week on "Sunday Morning" (actually, even more insisted they heard me all the time on "Morningside"). And when I recorded *Unexpected*, a mainly romantic album, record stores often filed it under "comedy."

By the time Stuart McLean, then "Sunday Morning"'s producer, called in the spring of 1983 to make me an offer, I was about ready to bow to the inevitable. How would I like to write a song a week about the Tory leadership convention, he asked. I decided it would be a good idea and said I'd do it if they'd also hire Doug Wilde, my music director, to accompany me on keyboards. Pushed to the wall by my hard bargaining, Stuart said okay. Hell, as they say, froze over.

(One problem I'd had with "Sunday Morning" the first time around was that I'd had to accompany myself on piano and I am, as Mr. Wilde charitably puts it, "instrumentally challenged.")

After the Tory leadership campaign was over, I continued writing songs for the show, but only one at a time and only every two or three weeks. I work mainly with Doug Wilde, and our producer is usually the international affairs editor Bob Carty. Thus, I get to hang out in a studio with two guys named Bob and Doug, and surely that's the dream of every young woman who's ever watched "Second City."

Carty is a singer-songwriter, speaks Spanish (I've always liked that in an hombre) and is very simpatico. He gives me the topics and some of the best lines. Occasionally we break down and call Doug Grant, who left "Sunday Morning" for the lure of "The Journal," to come back and let us pick his brain. Once again, Bob and Doug. It's the Canadian way, I guess.

I need this help because I'm not, as many people think, a news junkie looking for targets to pounce on. Left to my own devices I read the entertainment and feature pages, the fillers, and the (blush) household hints. Sorry about that.

I think that what I do is bring a common-sense point of view to the stories I tackle. The songs are based on news items everyone's reading. When we read these things I hope most of us say, "wait a minute, who do they think they're kidding?" I just take that thought, expand it a little and set it to music. (Once in a while Doug Wilde will also work on the tune.)

Sometimes I can't do it. Can't find a topic, can't find an angle. When this happens, I take a pass on the whole thing. My ambition just isn't all that burning and heaven forbid I should find myself in a higher tax bracket, helping subsidize the bail-out of some big corporation.

Some of the songs in this collection were not written for "Sunday Morning." A few, such as "What Should I Wear to the Revolution?" and "Andy and Koo's Duet," were actually inspired. Generally, the inspired ones aren't any better than the ones commissioned and written to a looming deadline. A hack is a hack is a hack, I believe.

Only one song, "Happy Can," comes from the several hundred written during my first stint at "Sunday Morning." Someone can look up the rest after I sell my papers to a university. (Pity Rochdale closed down.)

And this collection doesn't contain any of my romantic ballads, the songs on Latin American themes that were my obsession for a couple of years, or the more serious political material.

This is a book of the topical songs. It certainly doesn't cover everything that went on in Canada in the early eighties, but it is, I think, a little taste of our times.

I hope you enjoy it.

Nancy White
March 1986

Jacques S. LeDoux Speaks

Allô, allô, mes enfants in the literary world. My name is Jacques S. LeDoux and I am the garçon-secrétaire of Nancy White and she has asked me to write an introduction to her great oeuvre.

"Quel honneur, madame," I said to her. "May I see the first draft?"

She laughed that irritating laugh that makes people turn around and stare at her when she goes to the theatre.

"Jacques, mon petit bout de choux," she trilled. "It is not that simple. First I've got to apply for a Canada Council grant so I can go to Greece to write the book. Then I've got to buy a word processor and have it shipped over. *Then* I can create this work, no problem. You want to come with me, or will you stay in Toronto and come by twice a day to feed my cat?"

Thoughts of the famished face of the fishy-eyed feline made something rise into my Gallic gorge. "Je t'accompagne, chérie, bien sûr," I said quickly.

And that is how I got to spend five years on a Greek island with the bitch goddess of the north. It was formidable. I would say more, but that story, well, it's going to be *my* book. I'm looking for a title. Too bad *Les Miserables* is taken.

Drat.

Jacques S. LeDoux
March 1986

Lifestyle

I once found myself in a hot tub in Winnipeg with two ten-year-old boys. (Don't ask.) One of them looked at my floating feet and asked his friend, "Why do girls paint their toenails?"

The friend, wise beyond his years, replied, "It's a lifestyle."

"Lifestyle" is one of those unpleasant new words that came into vogue about the same time the words "parent" and "party" turned into verbs.

Now that I think of it, "lifestyle" was the journalistic term used to replace "women's section" in newspapers when we strident feminists wrote in to say we didn't like to be labelled as the readers of the fluffy stuff therein.

Of course, it's the most interesting part of the paper, let's face it. So all the songs in this chapter are about things that might appear in that section.

First, a song about the habits of the North American bourgeoisie in the eighties. Forgive me, it has "the Y word" in it, and I know people are sick of it. But I wrote it in August 1984, before it had been done to death by the media.

Yuppies, in case you've been off the planet for a looooong time, are Young Urban Professionals. Much has been written about their consuming and living habits, their penchant for physical fitness, gourmet foods, French immersion courses, and personal computers.

Now here is a sordid confession about the writing of this song. Everyone's favourite line is almost a direct quote from (gasp, wheeze) the dreaded right-wing journalist Barbara Amiel. In an interview in *Toronto Life Fashion* (which of course I didn't buy, OK? I, um, found it in a limo), Ms. Amiel is quoted as saying, "The only way you can sum up dating a younger man is, who wants to spend her life holding her stomach in. . . ."

15

Nancy with Professional Help in July 1981. Kneeling: Henry Heillig, Matt Zimbel; sitting: Doug Wilde, Lorne Nehring. This picture was taken in P.E.I., after a swim and with no makeup.

Photo: Andy Zimbel

Yuppie Love

If you sandblast my house
I'll wax your BMW,
If you sandblast my house,
I might even broil a fish for you,
And Janis and Jimi[1]
Will smile down from above
As we fall in yuppie love.

I'm gonna be
A little older than you,
I'm gonna be
In middle management too,
And if you marry me
And make me your wife,
I'll hold my stomach in
The rest of my life.

Yuppie love, it ain't no different,
Just a little more secure,
I can work on our relationship
While I get a manicure,
And though our yuppie love
    is deep and strong
I feel completely free,
It's easier to get away
From a two-car family.

And I will have our baby
When I'm forty-nine,
I'll have to stay in bed five months to do it,
But little Sasha will be fine,
And all the other parents
Will think it's kind of sweet
To watch my little boy
Help me cross the street.

Yuppie love, it ain't no different,
Just a little more secure,
I can work on our relationship
While I get a manicure,
And though our yuppie love
    is deep and strong
I feel completely free,
It's easier to get away
From a two-car family.

(Why, I'm so fit, I could probably *jog*
the fifteen hundred miles to
my mother's place.)

---

1. Janis Joplin and Jimi Hendrix

Nancy never looked like this and she never smoked, but she loves this picture.

Bob Carty called me early in 1986 about doing a new song for "Sunday Morning."

"There's two possibilities," he said. "Ronnie and Mikhail and the televised messages, or sex in Newfoundland."

Well, what would interest *you* more?

That day, Chris Brookes had come dashing into "Sunday Morning"'s luxurious offices waving the new issue of *Maclean's* and exclaiming "Second year in a row! Second year in a row!"

Yes, once again, Newfoundlanders had rated themselves more sexually active and more satisfied than people in any other province. Being a Newfoundlander, Brookes was pleased with this news.

No other details were given (except that Quebeckers rated themselves least satisfied – and best looking), so I called up Ron Gillis, a trained sociologist who was at Dalhousie University with Chris Brookes and me in the sixties.

Sometimes a scholarly perspective is helpful, and I thought the fact that Gillis is from P.E.I. and full of Atlantic lore would mean he could interpret the data in a truly meaningful way.

He had several theories. One had to do with dissatisfied Newfoundlanders moving to the mainland. One was about rubber boots and sheep. One was about lowered expectations. One was about time zones.

We may never know.

Hubba Hubba
Newfoundland

What makes a Newfoundlander so sexy?
What makes her feel so satisfied?
Is it the cod roe?
Is it the undertow?
The pull of that North Atlantic tide?
Is it pride?

What makes a Newfoundlander
    so "active"?
What is it makes him go like a mink?
Is it the spare time
That leads to the stair climb?
Or maybe these days he can't afford
    to drink?
Whatcha think?

All over the world the news is
    getting around,
And all the pleasure seekers are
    Newfoundland-bound;
Peckford will encourage this search
    for romance,
He's opening a Club Med in
    Come-by-Chance!
    (Come-by-chance?
        Obviously a misnomer!)

What makes the Newfs so very
    hot-blooded?
What gives them all that sensual skill?
Please spare me the cheap jokes,
The rubber boots and sheep jokes,
It's simply that they have more time
    to seek that thrill,
Cause they've always got that
    extra half an hour to kill.[1]

    (Listen, my dear, there's thirty
minutes till "The Journal" comes on.
What say I slips into something a little
more comfortable and we try some of
that famous Newfoundland fore and aft
play . . .)

---

1. For the benefit of any non-Canadians reading this, the province of Newfoundland on Canada's east coast is in a time
zone of its own, with a half-hour rather than an hour difference from its neighbours. CBC programs are always being
announced as being "half an hour later in Newfoundland." This is a strictly Canadian expression, something like
"Snow again, I didn't get your drift."

I get asked to do a lot of benefits. It's not because of my big heart, I can assure you. It's because I'm perceived as a political singer.

Boys and girls! Do not allow people to put this label on you; it leads to all sorts of trouble.

The big problem is wardrobe.

For instance, if I am singing at a concert for the Patriarchy Sucks League in Charlottetown, they may be politically offended if I wear my tarty little black dress and the industrial mascara.

If Baboons for Social Responsibility is the sponsor, they may not like me to wear leather pants. And leather pants pack better than anything.

And you see, politically correct clothing can be pretty drab for stage.

I always tell audiences that Joan Baez wrote the song about all this, but of course I lie. It was me, in a fit of creativity in October 1982, making fun of people like me who tend to get involved in supporting revolutions in Latin America while overlooking social problems at home.

Well, face it, it's more inspiring to shout "¡hasta la victoria final!" than mumble "it's time for another royal commission."

What Should I Wear
to the Revolution?

What should I wear to the revolution?
Is it déclassé to dress like Ché?
What should I wear to the revolution?
Should I wear socks with my Birkenstocks?
Now corduroy I find it always tends
    to wear so thin,
And olive green, quite frankly,
    doesn't do much for my skin!
What should I wear to the revolution?
Hey, *Mother Jones*, what's your solution?

What should I wear to the war
    of the classes?
Will I feel more struggly if I dress ugly?
Should I try hard to blend in
    with the masses?
Will crimplene pants rate a second glance?
Have you noticed as you're studying
    how revolution flowers,
Other people's masses look much
    better than ours!
What should I wear to the revolution?
Hey, Ed Broadbent, what's your solution?

What should I wear when we take
    to the hills?
Should I bring batches of elbow patches?
When we exercise our collective wills,
Will I fight better in a cashmere sweater?
Now silk gets torn so badly when you're
    crawling on your belly,
And polyester T-shirts get so smelly!
What should I wear to the revolution?
Hey, Jane Fonda, what's your solution?

(So I called up Jane Fonda and she
came to the phone and said (pant pant
pant pant), "Oh, hi, Nance. Listen, it's
no problem. You should always dress
exactly as I do and you'll be politically
correct at all times." I said, "Jane, don't
give me that. The last time I wore leg
warmers on a march, they fell down
around my ankles in the first block. It
was sooo embarrassing." She said "yes, I
know, it happens to me too. But we
always try to make it work *for* us. We
get two of the shorter compañeros to
march alongside me and hold them up as
a symbol of solidarity.")

Photo: Trish Wilde

"*Now silk gets torn so badly when you're
crawling on your belly.*"

"Me and my old man we don't go out much any more."

Photo: Trish Wilde

Several years ago, CITY TV in Toronto took advantage of the fitness craze and started an exercise show that became quite controversial. It's called "The Twenty-Minute Workout" and it *is* a little saucy. Three beautiful, young, and frighteningly fit women do aerobics and call out the commands in breathy little voices.

Some columnists complained the show was "soft porn," and that viewers just watched and didn't exercise. I suspect these people haven't seen much porn lately!

I know lots of people who actually do the exercises. Indeed, I made the big sacrifice myself twice before writing this song. It is indeed a workout. Whew. That's why on the recorded version of this song (see *The Sunday Morning Tapes*), Rick Whitelaw, Doug Wilde, and I added a panting track. Musica verité.

Twenty Minute Sit-It-Out

Me and my old man we don't go out
  much any more,
Movies cost too much and going bowling
  is a bore!
But when it comes to our TV
  we've got such discipline,
The "Twenty-Minute Workout" keeps us
  in the shape we're in.

And it's "eight more, six more,
  four more and two,
Touch your toes, blow your nose,
You can do it, good for you."
Sitting with my feet up, I'm basking
  in their praise,
I could do this workout for
  days and days and days!

We watch their perfect bodies doing
  things we'll never do,
Their routine goes on and on,
  my husband sees it through,
But by the time I run upstairs and
  put the outfit on,
Pour myself a cooling beer,
  the twenty minutes are gone!

And it's "four more, three more,
  two more, and one,
Work it out, stretch it out,
  aren't we having fun!"
In my mind I'm slender and as fit as I can be,
The "Twenty Minute Workout"
  women do it all for me.

In taverns of the nation, the patrons
  sip their beers,
Some of them hold records,
  they haven't moved in years,
But "Participaction" pushers can
  claim a victory,
Cause the "Twenty Minute Workout"
  is the show they want to see.

And it's "eight more, six more, five more,
  and four,
Keep your chins up, fellows,
  just two minutes more."
We love to see the legwarmers and
  watch the ladies sweat,
The "Twenty Minute Workout,"
  I swear I'll try it yet.

And it's "eight more, six more, four
  more, two more, zero more, minus
  two more, that's it, that's good! –
  Don't forget to breathe!"

In Los Angeles there's a tourist agency called "Pretentious Travel" – the perfect place for the character who sings this song to do business.

I wrote it for *The Last Virgin on the Planet*, a cabaret show I did with Doug Wilde at the Blue Angel in Toronto in June 1981. It was directed by the brilliant Ray Whelan for Open Circle Theatre. Opening night I heard him tell a friend, "Well, I knew I couldn't turn Nancy into Sarah Bernhardt but we did our best."

To set up this song, I came out in a huge picture hat and told the audience that although I travelled widely, I never went as a tourist. Rather I liked to "immerse myself in the culture of the peasants – eat their food, ride on the buses with the chickens and the babies, and so on."

"For instance," I went on, "last winter my 'compañero' and I visited Cuba, where we settled into a charming little village named Santa Maria del Mar. We discovered that what the natives do there is, they snorkel, ride bicycles, and boogie all night to pulsating Cuban rhythms. So of course, that's what we had to do.

"And I said to my compañero, 'Cumpa, it's no wonder their revolución was sooooo successful!'"

Of course many people in the audience knew that Santa Maria del Mar is just a tourist resort and that two weeks on the "playa" (beach) and many trips to Havana on the "guagua" (bus) didn't constitute a deep look at Cuban life.

Apart from the attitude of the song, most of the experiences in it were my own, including the confiscation of the camera. Actually, they only cut out a piece of the film. And I didn't sell my jeans. No one asked.

(Oh, and a cocodrilo is a crocodile.)

I Know Cuba

When I travel, I'm not a tourist, not me,
I am more like a student of
   "the school of life," you'll agree,
I live like the natives live
   when I go on vacation,
Taking the pulse, so to speak,
   of my fortunate host nation.

Two weeks on the "playa,"
   many trips on the "guagua,"
Sat around on the sand,
I know Cuba like the back of my hand.
Two weeks by the ocean,
   changed my money to pesos,
Heard a real Cuban band,
I know Cuba like the back of my hand.

Reds and rums and ration books,
Conga lines and curious looks,
I've been in cabs that had no brakes
And I've had the sugar shakes,
People ask if I saw Fidel,
Well, he called me twice, but what the hell,
He wanted to show me Old Havana,
But I had a date at the Tropicana.
   Socialism with spangles,
   If it don't sparkle, it dangles,
   We saw how the real Cubans live! –
   Real Cubans sing:
"Guantanamera, guajira, Guantanamera,
Guantanamera, guajira, Guantanamera,"[1]
   – constantly!

Went without peanut butter,
   sold my jeans to a native,
Got beautifully tanned,
I know Cuba like the back of my hand.
My confidence faded when my
   camera was confiscated,
But the officers treated me grand,
I know Cuba like the back of my hand.
Like the back, like the back, like the back,
   like the back of my hand!

("Ladies and gentlemen, we are now
approaching the crocodile farm where
you will pass a good time visiting the
hundreds of cocodrilos. At the time of
the Bay of Pigs were only two cocodrilos
in Cuba and they were very poor. But
Fidel, she gave them this nice farm and a
dental plan and now they can all read. Of
course, they are not allowed to leave,
but, why would they want to? And so,
please to pass a good time visiting the
cocodrilos but don't get too close. They
don't like very much the gringos.
Gracias, Thank you. Merci.")

"Cuba, que linda es Cuba,
   quien la defiende la quiere mas,
Cuba, que linda es Cuba,
   quien la defiende la quiere mas."[2]

---

1. Poem by José Martí, music by Hector Angulo and Pete Seeger.
2. "Cuba, how lovely is Cuba; he who defends her loves her more." This song is played all the time for tourists in Cuba, but the singers tactfully omit the line "now, without the Yankees, I like it more."

Here is a song about one of the things that unites Canadians coast to coast. Well, perhaps not in B.C.

Unhappy Motoring

Oh the blowers and the sanders
  and the salters are out
And the highway is white where
  the snow whirls about,
If you weren't sure it's Canada,
  now you've no doubt
As you wait for the Motor League to come.

Your engine is dead as an engine can be,
It's like you and your car have a
  shared misery
And the touch of the cables will
  set you both free
As you wait for the Motor League to come.

I seem to spend my days –
  in unproductive ways,
Winter just seems to bring –
  unhappy motoring,
In curious habitats –
  phone booths and laundromats,
I wait for the Motor League to come.

To the gods of the highway
  you're making your vow
That you'll get a new battery and
  you pray that somehow
Your old car won't get pranged
  by a passing snowplough
As you wait for the Motor League to come.

Now some say Canadians are
  an uncultured crew,
That our songs are derivative and
  our dances are few,
But, by God, there is one thing
  we know how to do
And that's wait for the Motor League
  to come.

If there's too much life and not enough style in your lifestyle, you may find yourself in the world of social workers. Social workers are like ballet dancers – they have a short, intense, pain-ridden career, and then burn out.

It's the system, the bureaucracies, the caseloads, the cutbacks. Perhaps most of all, it's having your ideals bashed about day after day.

The "Mrs. Linda" of the song is my friend and one-time manager Linda Grobovsky, the most compassionate person in the world, hence a perfect candidate for social worker burnout. The stories in the song are hers.

Mrs. Linda

Oh they call her "Mrs. Linda,"
Because they can't pronounce her name,
And they are driving Mrs. Linda
Out of the social worker game.

CHORUS:
And another social worker burns out,
   burns out,
A compassionate person walks out,
   walks out,
It's just too much, no thanks, no more,
She's seen it, she's heard it, she's had it.

"Oh, Mrs. Linda, I got discharged today,
So get me a job and a place to stay,
Give me some money, cure my disease,
   and take my husband, please."
"Mrs. Linda, I got a gun here,
I'm not having any fun here,
And I know where you live, Mrs. Linda,
I'm coming over now."

"He put me in the hospital,
I got no money and the hostel's full,
It's years he's been beating me
   black and blue,
Mrs. Linda, what should I do?"
Mrs. Linda's trying not to stare,
The stories curl Mrs. Linda's hair,
She keeps her cool, she is the diplomat,
She says "How do you *feel* about that?"

"Oh, Linda, step into my office, please,
I guess you've heard about the
   funding freeze,
We'll have to cut back, and by the way,
You get eight new clients today."

Nancy being interviewed by Gary Dunford for The Canadian Composer, *1978.*

"When the Wino" is a confession song, and it's about a dilemma I share with a lot of well-meaning folk – how to deal with panhandlers.

The wino encounter represents the only occasion when I'm pleased by sexist behaviour. If I'm walking down the street with a guy, the wino will usually approach *him* rather than me. It's a satisfactory trade-off. I think the wino is marginal because he's been drunk for thirty years. He thinks I'm marginal because I'm a woman. Seems fair.

A couple of notes: The NDP, Canada's New Democratic Party, is a fine organization noted for its excellent taste in music. (They have booked me to sing at several conventions.) And "Touch the Earth" was a CBC radio folk music show which ran a commercial that always annoyed me: "We talk to the real people – the winos and the hookers . . ." (as opposed to we phonies who pay income tax, I suppose.)

When the Wino

I am a kneejerk liberal, I vote for the NDP,
And I love to go and picket at the
   U.S. Embassy,
And I get called "progressive,"
   but that's not what they would say
If they could read my mind
When the wino comes my way.

Cause you're damned if you do and
   you're damned if you don't.
You're a fool if you give and
   a meanie if you won't.
Oh you just can't win and you always pay
When the wino comes your way.

Well he comes weaving over,
   he looks filthy, red, and sick,
And I'm praying to that wino god it won't
   be me he'll pick,
Cause I don't believe that
   "Touch the Earth"-y-wise-old-wino
   myth,
Well, let me put it this way, he's not
   the first person I'd choose to be stuck
   between floors
in an elevator with.

Cause you're damned if you do and
   you're damned if you don't.
You feel like you've been had if you give
   and such a grinch if you won't.
Aw you just can't win and you always pay
When that wino comes your way.

When I first came into this town,
   they often caught my eye.
Then I grew a Toronto face and
   now they mostly pass me by.
But they just can't be avoided,
   falling off those downtown curbs.
And with all this renovation,
   they're migrating to the burbs.

But you're damned if you do and
   you're damned if you don't
You're a fool if you give and
   a meanie if you won't
You just can't win and you always pay
When that wino comes your way.

The first folk festival I ever played was in Sudbury, the gutsy Northern Ontario mining town. I've sung there several times since and have always been knocked out by the people and the festival. It's the only bilingual festival in the country, and the Sudbury people switch back and forth from English to French with amazing grace. Many of them are so bilingual you can't tell if French or English is their mother tongue.

For several years of my life I wanted to *be* French Canadian. It didn't seem to be possible, but I worked at it a bit. Later on I wanted to be Latin American, and I worked at that too. It's my theory that because we English Canadians have not much of a culture of our own, we can adopt any other culture in the world and get into it. I once toured with an actor who sang Bulgarian folk songs on the bus. I know he wanted to *be* Bulgarian. Perfectly understandable to me.

At any rate, during my French period, I picked up enough of the langue to write a half French song – a tribute to Sudbury.

In Sudbury

In Sudbury ils parlent français,
In the middle of the sentence
   ils peuvent switcher,
Je me sens confuse, confused, you bet,
In Sudbury, je m'appelle "Nanette,"
In Sudbury je me sens chez moi,
They're always fighting for leurs droits,
Ils font la grève, they go on strike,
Les gens du nord, sont les gens I like.

Gens I like, gens I like.
. . . Let's see, I like Jean-Paul, Jean-Claude,
   Jean-Pierre, Jean-Luc, Ti-Jean,
     Grand-Jean, . . . et Bernard.

Je rêve la nuit de Sudbury,
It does such crazy choses to me,
The northern lights, the Boréal,
Sophistiqué like Montréal,
Does INCO really give a damn
For the miners' lives et la lutte des femmes,
Pour sa musique et son esprit
Que vive les gens du Sudbury!

Sudbury, Sudbury,
Que vive les gens du Sudbury!
Long live solidarity,
Que vive les gens du Sudbury!

A peace picnic on the Toronto Islands, June 1984.

J'adore chanter à Sudbury,
Les gens sont sympathiques to me,
I can't explique this mystery,
Je parle français comme John Crosbie.
But in the air il y a quelque chose,
The scent of nickel, I suppose,
Pour sa musique et son esprit,
Que vive les gens du Sudbury!

Sudbury, Sudbury,
vive les gens du Sudbury!
Long live solidarity,
vive les gens du Sud – bu – reeeeee.

This was taken one summer at the Manitoulin Island Folk Festival. The unicorn has some connection with a Morris Dancers' video. Best not to ask.

Canadians move more than people in most countries. Possibly it's because we're never sure we've made the right choice of community. The grass is always greener, jobs always better, somewhere else.

For many of us, the grass is greenest in Vancouver. The mountains, the ocean, lush forests, happy vegetarians, Paul Horn recording duets with whales – it's all too enticing. I often think I'd like to live there.

Then of course the spectre of food banks, rain, and bizarre Socred practices rears its head, and I decide to stay put in Toronto.

I wrote "Ah, Lotusland," which expresses this geographic dilemma, when Leonard Schein booked me to do a concert at the Ridge Theatre in Kitsilano.

Ah, Lotusland

Ah, Lotusland,
You call to me from over the mountains!
Ah, Lotusland,
I long to see your flowers and fountains!
But I like pollution and I like the rush,
I like the crowding and I like the crush
Of my city that grows and carries on
On the banks of the stagnant River Don.[1]

Ah, Lotusland,
I love your trees and all of that shrubbery,
But ah, Lotusland,
I think of skis, my knees get rubbery,
But I like granola and I like the sea,
I like the memory of the NDP,
I could buy me a futon and snort cocaine
And enrol in that course where they
    teach you how to not even notice
    the rain![2]

Ah, Lotusland,
Could I endure your changeable weather?
I ask myself,
Could whales and I be happy together?
But I know my nature and I know my place,
And some of us rats gotta stay in the race,
But I'd think about moving to Van
    some day
If they just wouldn't tow my car away,[3]
And maybe I'd think about starting to pack
If they'd promise to bring
    Dave Barrett back,
If the sun would come out
    ("it's so nice when it's bright"),
If the Ridge could show movies
    after midnight![4]
Well the answer just came to me
    while I was stoned,
Gonna call Dave Suzuki,[5]
    gonna get myself cloned!
Nothing to fear,
I'd be there, I'd be here,
Here's to you,
Love to you,
Lotusland.

1. This would be your Toronto, Ontario.

2. That's what they say in Vancouver. "Oh, we don't even notice it." I think it's because they prepare; at the Vancouver Folk Festival everyone brings ground sheets and ponchos. To be fair, I've been at the festival several years when it didn't rain at all.

3. They will tow away your car in Vancouver when your meter expires.

4. The first time I played there the Ridge had just lost a battle to be allowed to show late-night films.

5. Dr. David Suzuki is our most famous geneticist.

And now, let's hear it for the wealthy. They just don't get celebrated in song half enough.

In the spring of 1985, workers at six Eaton's stores in the Toronto area had been on strike almost half a year. Their demands were small and the store was being completely obnoxious. People in the arts community wanted to express support for the strikers. Rick Salutin, the playwright, got a group of us together, and we met with people from the unions and organized a benefit concert at Massey Hall.

It was a sensational night – a great show, a great audience, a full house.

We discovered that the late Lady Eaton had herself sung at Massey Hall in 1920, "assisting" the great Canadian tenor Edward Johnston by singing several songs in a benefit concert. (Is there any other kind?)

I thought, what if Lady Eaton were to come to our show and haunt the venue with a little song? What would she sing? And I wrote and sang "I'm Glad That I Don't." It's a Gilbert and Sullivanish number, and I was accompanied on piano and synthesizers by Doug Wilde and his brother James, keyboard players from Sault Ste. Marie. This allowed me to express my thanks to "the Wildes of North Ontario," something I'd been longing to say. I sing this song in a hideous operatic voice. I figure if the opera singers will insist on massacring pop songs at every opportunity, we pop singers should get even.

Bob and Doug. "Sunday Morning" producer Bob Carty and Nancy's music director/accompanist Doug Wilde work out the arrangement for some brilliant little song or other. 1986.

I'm Glad that I Don't

When winter dies and spring has sprung,
My blood boils up and I feel quite young,
I almost want to go outside
So I ask the maid to open the
   windows wide.
I call for my car and I go downtown,
I buy a hat, I buy a gown,
And though my life can be a bore,
I'm glad that I don't work at
   Timothy's store.
CHORUS: She's glad that she don't work
   at Timothy's store.

For the girls who work at Timothy's store
Spend a lifetime on the floor.
They work very hard and they never fuss,
And we think it kind of them to work for us.
But a woman's goal is to catch a man,
And entertain, and start a clan,
My feet are never swelled and sore,
I'm glad that I don't work at
   Timothy's store.
CHORUS: She's glad that she don't work
   at Timothy's store.

When it's winter in the city,
And the streets are grey and shitty,
I'm glad that I don't have to go on strike,
For your feet hurt when you picket,
And I'd get too cold to stick it,
And walking unescorted isn't very ladylike!

Oh life is good in Toronto,
I feel at home wherever I go,
I leave my troubles in the lurch
And steal away to sing at
   Timothy's church. [1]
Now the girls at the store,
   they want fair pay,
My husband says, "Ha ha, no way,"
He'll have to show those girls the door,
I'm glad that I don't work, I'm glad that
   I don't work, I'm glad that I don't work
   at Timothy's store.

I'm one big spender, My city, my centre,
I'm one big spender, My city, my centre! [2]

---

1. I grew up in Charlottetown, P.E.I., where churches had names like St. James's and St. Peter's, so I was quite shocked to learn that one of the most famous churches in Toronto was Timothy Eaton Memorial. After I'd lived here awhile I realized that, really, it was quite appropriate.

2. "My city, my centre" is the slogan of the enormous Eaton Centre in Toronto. It's right around the corner from Massey Hall, where we did our show.

A 1984 publicity shot.

Here's a song for new mothers. It's a touch personal, but with some universal applications, and it includes a veiled plea for mercy to the general public.

Have you ever been pregnant? I was pregnant in 1985, and there were lots of surprises. The big shock is loss of privacy. I was constantly floored by the nerve of strangers. I am, like Margaret Trudeau, a private person, and it always amazed me when someone I didn't know said "When are you due?" Or when a nodding acquaintance placed a proprietary hand on my stomach.

I decided the answer would be to wear one of those adorable T-shirts with "BABY" and a down-pointing arrow on it, cross out "BABY" and paint "OVARIAN CYST" in its place. This might encourage diplomacy, I thought.

I didn't do it, of course, because I was trying to keep a low profile. Fat chance, ha ha.

I wrote "It's So Chic" to sing at the Preggae Woman fitness class Christmas party. I also did it for relatives on Christmas day. Otherwise, it's been unsung and unheard.

It's a banjo tune.

It's So Chic (to be Pregnant at Christmas)

It's so chic to be pregnant at Christmas,
I feel like the round yon virgin of yore,
Although I have a warm bed to sleep in
There's no room for me when I go
   to the store,
Cause the aisles are so narrow
   and crowded,
Christmas shopping has never been
   such a pain,
Oops, here comes another
   Braxton Hicks contraction[1]
And we're knocking over
   knick-knacks again.

The salesclerks are so friendly
   this Christmas,
One said "Oh God, lady, don't you
   have it here,"
Their discretion and manners go
   right out the door
When I and my stomach appear,
People like to put their hands on
   my fundus,[2]
And they want to know *exactly*
   when it's due,
I say "Why do you care, are you planning
   to be there?
I could use an extra labour coach or two."

I am such fun at a party,
Trying hard to get high on life,
Desperately avoiding the smokers,
Being introduced as someone's wife.

I enjoy being pregnant at Christmas,
Though my identity is draining away,

If I ever get asked my opinion again,
I'll simply smile and continue to crochet,
It's so Biblical to be pregnant
   at Christmas,
No matter what stories you believe,
And I may suffer from gravid senilis[3]
   (and heartburn and nausea and
charleyhorses and frequent micturation
and varicose veins and shortness of
breath and hiatus hernia and a burning
rash on the sternum and popping in the
ears and that tired achy feeling in the
groin . . .)
But I won't be alone on New Year's Eve.

---

1. This is a contraction of the uterus that happens a lot
   in late pregnancy. It doesn't hurt, it just feels very
   tight and weird.

2. The pregnant woman quickly acquires a rich new
   vocabulary. The fundus is the top part of the
   pregnant belly. By the way, people I know *well* never
   laid a glove on it.

3. Gravid senilis was my favourite pregnancy term. It
   lets you off the hook again and again. It refers to the
   senility that comes with pregnancy. You see, for the
   whole term all you can think of is this miracle that's
   happening, so then when you're on stage and forget
   some lyrics of a song you've sung a hundred times,
   it's perfectly okay. The rest of the things are what
   they call "minor symptoms" of pregnancy. They drive
   you crazy but doctors just say, "Hey, man, you're
   pregnant, anything can happen." "Micturation" is a
   nasty word for peeing. "Hiatus hernia" means there's
   this valve that's not closing properly and so you
   sometimes regurgitate . . . but you don't want the
   details. I had all these symptoms at one time or
   another except the varicose veins. But it was a good
   trade-off. I no longer got migraines, and didn't have to
   try to memorize my lines.

Before the baby was born I was asked to review a new prenatal product on CBC Radio's "Dayshift." It was a cassette of Baroque music designed to be played to one's baby *in utero*. The idea was that the baby would get to know the tunes and, when no longer *in utero*, would respond to them by relaxing and sleeping.

I decided that if I were going to spend my time conditioning the poor little creature (I mean, if she doesn't *like* Baroque music, what defence does she have???), I would also send her a message about her parents' expectations for her.

So I wrote these lyrics to a tune by Boccherini and did the song on "Sunday Morning" as well as on "Dayshift."

It worked really well. The baby typed this manuscript for me.

Memo to Droola[1]

(Sung to the tune of String Quartet in E,
Op. 13, No. 5, "Minuetto" by Boccherini)

You will be a lawyer, and make the
  megabuck,
You'll support your mommy when she's
  down on her luck,
You will read at two,
We'll be proud of you,
And you must promise not to sniff the glue.

You will be the star of French immersion
  nursery school,
When you are a week old, we'll hit
  the swimming pool,
I'll flash the cards, you see,
  for your vocabulary,
You'll get voice-over work before
  you're three.

When you cry and fuss
We'll do some calculus,
When your teeth come in
We'll get you modellin'.

I will keep you on the breast 'til
  you are five or six,
There's no little problem that mother's
  milk can't fix,
You will march for peace,
You'll never get obese,
And you will be my brothers'
  favourite niece.

Promise me delight,
Sleep right through the night,
Don't be colicky,
Don't throw up on me.

I will take you shoppin', and dress you
  for success,
Then over at the drop-in, we'll play
  a game of chess,
At the age of three
You'll write a symphony,
But please include a banjo part for me.

And some rainy day
When you're feeling blue,
Your dad and I will buy
a MacIntosh for you.

We will have a perfect birth 'cause
  I am super-fit,
They'll offer epidural but I'll have
  no need of it,
If the music's right,
We will bond that night,
And you'll begin a life of sheer delight.

---

1. "Droola" was our baby's *in utero* name.
After she emerged, we named her Suzannah.

Oh Those Tories

I've always liked the word "Tory." It makes me think of the old joke: "How do you top a car?" – "tep on the brake, tupid."

I also like Tory jokes. Someone once said that "Progressive Conservative" sounds like someone who likes to rev the engine in neutral.

Now Tory policy, that's something else again. I don't like to think about it too much.

The 1983 Tory leadership campaign was pretty interesting. The far right candidates said marvellous things. John Crosbie dazzled us with his theory that a unilingual candidate would be the best one to unite the country. Peter Pocklington dazzled us just by being Peter Pocklington.

The candidates campaigned hard and towards the end they were personally contacting delegates all over the country. My sympathies went out to those innocents, suddenly besieged in their own homes.

---

1. "Michael" is Mike Duffy of CBC TV's "The National." During the leadership campaign, Brian Mulroney was in the habit of calling TV newscasters and complaining if he didn't like their coverage, and at one point he threatened to sue Mike Duffy (sue Mike Duffy!!!) over some trifle.

No Life at All

Oh the life of a Tory delegate,
They say it's no life at all,
Every time you turn around,
Another Tory comes to call,
They pull up in their limousines
And they call you by your name,
They stroll across your turnip patch
And go back the way they came.

Mulroney wants to sing to you
Some dreadful Irish song:
  "Michael, me boy, you done me wrong,
  I'll have your ass before too long."[1]
Wilson bores you one-on-one,
It takes just half as long,
Clark shakes your hand 'til it's bloodless,
He claims he's got the stuff,
Crombie wants to arm-wrestle,
To prove to you he's tough!

Oh the life of a Tory delegate,
They say it's no life at all,
There's Tories trampling your front lawn,
There's Tories in your hall.

(The other day there was a knock on
the door, and it's Peter Pocklington!
And he's got Wayne Gretzky with him.
And he says "I'm leaving Wayne with
you for the evening, and I hope I can
count on your support June 11." And he
left.
  And I'm thinking "What could I
possibly say to Wayne Gretzky? But

then I remembered what I read years ago
in "Calling All Girls Magazine" – always
ask a boy about himself. So I said, "So,
Wayne, how come you aren't running?
You've got the looks, the money, you're
good in the corners and vague on the
issues – you'd be perfect!" And he said
he had thought about it. He'd been
scouted by several factions of the party
and he knew he could win. But he said
he had the nagging feeling that no matter
how well he did, he might wake up one
morning and find he'd been traded to the
Socreds.
  Just then the phone rang. "Oh God," I
thought, "I know who that is. It's The
Breather from the East and his damn
translator." So I said "Allô, fiche-moi la
paix, you guys, je suis très occupée avec
le hockey." The translator says "She
says she's honoured to hear from you
Mr. Crosbie." Crosbie says "Tell her
'hello my dear can I count on your
support?'" Translator says "Monsieur
Crosbie dit 'Au secours, ma chère!'" I
decide to speak to Mr. Crosbie in his
own language. "John," I says, "I has one
word for you, and that's 'adieu,' and that
means 'bye bye,' bye.")

Oh the life of a Tory delegate,
They say it's no life at all,
Every time you turn around,
Another Tory comes to call.

During the campaign, candidates tried to outdo each other with stories of their humble beginnings. The winner hands down was Brian Mulroney, who not only got to be Tory leader, but prime minister as well. I have summed up just about all Mr. Mulroney's campaign policy in this song which, borrowing a title from the Monty Pythons, I call "Life of Brian." (I borrowed the tune from myself, actually. This piece of music started life as a Paul Anka-style-guy song called "I'm Incredible.")

Life of Brian

I started out small,
Just a working class guy,
I sang in the choir,
My little voice was so high,
I studied so hard,
Even drove me a truck,
I may be a lawyer, but you know,
I've rolled in the muck.
I started out small,
Didn't stay there for long,
I ran me a company,
I was rich, tall, and strong,
In a voice like Ron Reagan's,

There's a song I can sing you all,
And this is it, folks,
I'm bilingual.

Oui! I'm bilingual (bilingue, bilingue)
That's what they say (je suis bilingue)
In French or in English
   (vachement bilingue)
I'm a killer, c'est vrai (comme tout le gang)
A dimension of tenderness
And a budget I'll bring you all,
But most of all, mes chèrs amis,
I'm bilingual. (Just like Pierre.)

Although Mulroney as prime minister has tried to avoid formulating policy of any kind, he has, at least, a tendency. If I can put it charitably, it involves building on our friendship with the United States or, less charitably, "show me the spot, Ron, my lips are ready."

One of the Mulroney government's first moves was to abolish FIRA, the Foreign Investment Review Agency, which had tried to ensure that foreign investment would be beneficial to Canada, and replace it with something called Investment Canada which, I guess, hands out maps and keys to our cities.

In this song, I play the role of our entire country, inviting, nay begging, an old lover to come back home. It's okay, it's safe, the socialist hordes are gone. Come and get it!

My FIRA's Gone

Photo: Trish Wilde

"Won't you come back to me with your cowboy charm?"

Hello, big boy.
Oh, how I've missed you!
Won't you come back to me with
    your cowboy charm!
I always like a man
With a lot of cash in his jeans,
I feel so prosperous when I hang
    on your arm.

Hey there, Sammy,
My door is open wide;
The light is always on, and a welcome
    you'll find,
My FIRA's gone now,
I'm ready to take you in,
I won't ask no questions 'bout
    what's on your mind.

I'm only sorry I've no bananas to give you,
And I can't work cheap for you like
    your girl in Hong Kong,
But I'll be good to you, and you can
    rough me up a bit,
I know you like to do that, makes you feel
    big and strong.

So listen, hot shot,
When you coming over?
I can't wait much longer, I got rent to pay.
Baby, all I have is yours,
All I ask is a helping hand;
I wanna be your best friend,
And take you all the way.

The Tory government's first minister of defence was the Honourable Robert Coates. He didn't stay honourable for long!

   Mr. Coates got in trouble for visiting a strip joint in Lahr, Germany. There was a great concern in Canada about a breach of security. Coates did, after all, spend a long time chatting with a waitress. Tsk tsk.

   He resigned at the request of the prime minister, and we were all relieved. I mean, think of the beans he may have spilled to the young woman!

Canadian Secrets

A guy must beware when he's in his cups
If he's strong and influential,
Sometimes he doesn't know when
   he should shut up
And he gets all confidential,
And a girl in a bar always knows how to be
The world's best listener,
And I shudder to think of Canadian secrets
The minister might have told to her.

He might have given her
   Wayne Gretzky's number,
Or said "don't drink our wine,"
Or told her 'bout an Ottawa parking place
Where you never get a fine;
She might have passed on the formula
To our many enemies
For how we get that maple syrup
Out of the maple trees.

Canadian secrets concealed beneath
   the snow,
Canadian secrets the world would kill
   to know,
Canadian secrets concealed beneath
   the snow,
Canadian secrets the world would kill
   to know.

She could've been just a dancer,
Or she could've been some kind of a spy,
Or she could've been in charge
   of a smuggling ring
For Red Rose Tea and rye;
And he might have been charmed and
   dropped his guard
And spoken against his will,
Or let her see the handsome mounties
On a fifty dollar bill!

He might've given her Wayne
   Gretzky's address
Or Madame Benoit's recipe,
Or showed her the length
Of Lightfoot's "Railroad Trilogy"!
He might've let slip what schools
   were closed
In last year's winter storms,
Or, God forbid, the colours of the
   brand new uniforms.

("So, Dagmar, I've got the information.
The sailor boys will be in white, und the
army boys in green und the fly boys will
be in some kind of a blue – I don't know
what they call it. Then, he showed me a
strange document. It was red, and it had
on it a picture of thirty-two policemen. I
don't know if they were the top guys or
not, but I think so, because each one had
his own horse. He told me he could get
me a copy of this! Then, I tried to find
out from him how many Junos has Anne
Murray. But his lips were sealed. He is
one tough cookie, this one!)

Canadian secrets, concealed beneath
   the snow,
Canadian secrets the world would kill
   to know,
Canadian secrets, each more sordid than
   the one before,
Canadian secrets, the ammunition in the
   information war,
Canadian secrets.

Photo: Trish Wilde

"So, Dagmar, I've got the information . . ."

45

Brian Mulroney quickly developed a technique for dealing with scandals in his party. He attacked the accusers and spoke of the high esteem in which he held the accused.

Mulroney was in great form when his minister of justice (justice!) got into trouble. It was patronage again. Now nobody in Canada gets too upset over patronage. It is, after all, a grand old tradition. But the Tories had been very self-righteous about it during the election campaign.

So when the Hon. John Crosbie was reminded that his two lawyer sons had been given federal contracts in Newfoundland, both he and Mulroney became enraged. Crosbie called his questioner in the House of Commons "dastardly, despicable, scurrilous, and scurvy." When MP Sheila Copps asked another question he shot her a patronizing "quiet down baby." Mulroney pointed out that Mr. Crosbie was "a man of unimpeachable integrity." I thought it was a phrase that would sing well.

Publicity shot, 1983.

Photo: Normunds Berzins

46

Unimpeachable

Ask no questions, we'll tell you no lies
In the Tory party,
We believe in family ties
In the Tory party,
We like to care for our own,
Get their noses in The Trough,
And the Liberals may scoff,
But the P.M. explains to them:

"He's a man of unimpeachable integrity,
And his honour is unsullied and intact,
A man of unimpeachable integrity,
Who should never be examined
    or attacked,
There's no conflict of interest,
    that's not possible,
Surely you have to agree,
Because the minister's a man of
    unimpeachable integrity."

Are we old fashioned? Maybe.
In the Tory party,
We call our women "baby"
In the Tory party,
We like to patronize them so they'll
    never run again,
And the libbers may complain
But the P.M. can explain:

"He's a man of unimpeachable integrity
Whose honour is unsullied and intact,
A man of unimpeachable integrity
Who should never be examined
    or attacked,
That sexist remark wasn't meant that way,
Mila and I both agree,
Because the minister's a man
    of unimpeachable integrity,
He's unimpeachable, unreachable,
If Crosbie were a whale he'd be
    unbeachable,
A man of unimpeachable integ-ri-tee.
Like me."

I used to do a song called "Nous Sommes Des Enfants," about the paternalism of the Ontario Tory government under Bill Davis. Quite honestly, I thought I'd be able to sing that song forever.

But to everyone's amazement, the Davis dynasty ended in 1985. Mr. Davis resigned. "Sunday Morning" sentenced me to write a Bill Davis song, and I watched the Bill Davis testimonial film shown at the leadership convention. I swear, my arteries nearly hardened as I sat through that evening. Zzzzzzzzzz. Anyway, here is my petite chanson.

Photo: Trish Wilde

Nancy listens back during the recording of her album Unexpected *at Inception Sound in Toronto, January 1982.*

It's Been Bland

He loved the Argos, he loved the Jays,
He loved his family, like in the
  good old days,
He wasn't too left, he wasn't too right,
Reckon he slept pretty easy at night.

He's already filled a big place in the sky
Where unfinished sentences go
  when they die,
And answers he gave us, while smiling
  so nice,
Make Brian Mulroney sound clear
  and concise.

Bye, bye, Bill,
We're sad but we have no fear,
Having you gone
Will be just like having you here.

No scandal has touched him in all of
  this time,
He stayed in the game but stayed out
  of the slime,
He's a soother of feelings,
  a great compromiser,
A speech from our Bill makes
  a good tranquillizer.

He believed that the polls showed
  the right way to go,
'though they never ask me or
  the people I know,
But the ones who will live out their
  lives in his debt
Are the ones who'll watch baseball
  without getting wet.

Bye, bye, Bill,
We're sad but we have no fear,
Having you gone
Will be just like having you here.

They say that you always get
  what you deserve,
In Ontario voters he touched not a nerve,
Nothing was promised, and
  nothing was planned,
So adios, Bill, may we say it's been bland?

Bye, bye, Bill,
We're sad but we have no fear,
Having you gone
Will be just like having you here.

Bye, bye, Bill
Bye, bye, Bill
Bye, bye, Bill
So long Brampton Bill.

In September 1985, Canada celebrated one year of Brian Mulroney's Tory government, and "Sunday Morning" wanted a song of joy and gratitude.

I tried to get specific about Mulroney's achievements in the song but it wasn't easy. It had been a year of spectacular mind changing, and not a lot of action.

That was in terms of the country as a whole. But Brian had been a good MP, handing out many goodies to his own riding, Manicouagan, Quebec.

(My favorite Manicouagan story was about the fine prison being awarded, if that's the right verb, to the town of Port Cartier. It was announced the government would build a maximum security prison there for inmates who were in danger in other jails. The new jail would house child murderers, serial killers, and informers, but the town's mayor assured his citizens that "no nasty people will be coming here."

"It will be people with alcoholic personalities and informers. An informer is not a bad person," he elaborated.)

For "One Year of Mulroney," I stole a line from the casual conversation of "Sunday Morning" producer Steve Wadhams.

"What do you think of Mulroney anyway?" I asked him.

"I dunno," he answered, "there's something about him . . . it's that well-hung voice. . . ."
Indeed!

One Year of Mulroney

Nancy doesn't know which folk festival this is, what year it was taken, or who took it. She includes it to show that, although instrumentally challenged, she can accompany herself if pushed to the wall.

One year of Mulroney,
Let the banners fly,
Oh well, just three more years to
    election time, say I.

One year of achievement,
Glorious deeds were done,
Too bad we all don't live in Manicouagan.

One year of the rumble
Of the well-hung voice,
One year thinking "oh my God,
    this guy was our choice!"

One year of decision,
A year of Tory pride,
Hey, it's a decision when you decide
    not to decide.

So happy anniversary
To Mr. Brian Mulroney,
From those of us who're left at CBC,
We're lonely, but we love you.
    (And we love Mila too.)

One year of explaining
Ever so patiently,
Tory ministers can do anything 'cause
    they are
    men of unimpeachable integrity.

One year of trying
To give us away,
Twelve months of cozying up to the
    good ole U.S.A.

One year of Mulroney.
Let the banners fly . . .

Over the years I've made several fruitless attempts at writing Christmas songs. It's nearly impossible. But I did one for "Sunday Morning" in 1984 that was so festive we decided to run it again in 1985 with an updated lyric. So get out the sleigh bells and try to sing like a nasty little boy soprano on this number.

Tory Christmas 1984, 1985

1984:

1. It's a Tory kind of Christmas,
We must pay for how we've sinned,
It's a Tory kind of Christmas,
See us twisting in the wind,
Financial holes we're caulking,
There'll be coal in every stocking,
As we carol out the Christmas blues,
Santa wears a pink slip and running shoes.[1]

2. It's a Tory kind of Christmas,
There's blood upon the floor,
And the scientists who studied birds
Won't study them no more,
There's Christmas trees in flower,
But they're dumping solar power,[2]
As we carol out the Tory song,
Santa's gonna drop by, but not for long.

CHORUS:

So ring, ring the merry, merry bells
Throughout this land so fair and just,
Sing a song of universal brotherhood
that is a "sacred trust,"[3]
Tories! heed the pitiful cries
Of Tiny Ed and Tiny John,
Don't forget the awful day you promised
You would Bless Us, Every One.

3. It's a Tory kind of Christmas
When you work for the CBC,
They fired the Friendly Giant,
And the next one could be me,
The arts are just a frill, you know,
They've always been the first to go,[4]
So carol out the Christmas cheer,
Santa will be laid off this time next year.

---

1. During his election campaign, Brian Mulroney promised to trim a lot of fat from government and pledged that a lot of people would be handed "a pink slip and running shoes."

2. The new Tory government made serious cuts in the budget of the Ministry of the Environment.

3. Mulroney referred to the maintenance of social programs as a "sacred trust" and said they should never be tied to levels of income.

1985:

1. It's a Tory kind of Christmas,
In a Tory kind of year,
And many a loyal party friend
Received a nice career;
The Crosbie boys we won't forget,
Though neither is a Q.C. yet,[5]
As we carol out the Tory law,
Santa wears a blue suit in Ottawa.

2. It's a Tory kind of Christmas
With a Tory Christmas glow,
As the Reagans and Mulroneys meet
Beneath the mistletoe;
The friendship seems to blossom
And the prospects are just awesome,
As we carol out the Christmas song,
Santa's independent, but not for long.

3. It's a Tory kind of Christmas
When you work for the CBC,
It's lonely in the building,
Just like at the NFB,
The arts are just a frill you know,
They've always been the first to go,
As we carol out the Christmas cheer:
Santa will be cancelled this time next year.

Photo: Lindsay Lozon

Publicity photo, 1985.

4. I first wrote "the arts *is* just a frill you know, *it's* always been the first to go." You can choose whichever version pleases you grammatically. Just don't write to me about it, okay?

5. When Ontario premier David Peterson abolished the awarding of Q.C.s in the province, John Crosbie announced that, as federal minister of justice, he'd continue to give them out. I figure his lawyer sons are about due for that little perk.

Delicious Stories

The Ontario government kept a hangman on its payroll for *eight years* after capital punishment had been abolished. Just in case, you know.

That is my idea of a delicious story.

Natives of Papua, New Guinea, use pages from the Yellowknife newspaper *News North* to roll long thin cigarettes which they stick in their pierced nostrils, thus enabling themselves to work and smoke at the same time.

This is tasty.

Last year's Miss America, Susan Akin, revealed to the press that she sprays her bottom with Firm Grip to keep her bathing suit from riding up.

Mmmmmm.

These are the kind of stories I love. It gladdens my heart when Jerry Falwell comes back from South Africa and talks about how great their government is. It delights me to hear Mitzi Seaga, wife of the prime minister of Jamaica, tell an international conference, "We have no drug problem in Jamaica."

You don't have to go to the sleazy tabloids for these amazing stories, but you do have to go past page one sometimes.

The silly stories have inspired quite a few "Sunday Morning" songs. An early one marked the opening up of China to the West a few years back.

One of the first American companies to go into China was Coca Cola. Coke was marketed there under a Chinese name which, when transliterated into English, came out as "can mouth can happy." I wrote them this little jingle.

Publicity shot, around 1973.

Happy Can

Happy can, happy mouth,
Things go better, north and south,
When the thirst is quenched, you see,
It's easy to fight hegemony.

Happy mouth, happy can,
Wearing clothes by Pierre Cardin,
We'll show the world a big surprise,
Watch us westernize!

You like the Great Wall Discotheque?
You ain't seen nothing yet,
My comrade left the rice field
And bought a new Corvette,
We had a date on Friday,
And I survived, somehow,
Though he took me to McDonald's
For some fries and a Big Mao.

Happy me, happy you,
Goodbye, curtain of bamboo,
Hello, Yankee businessman,
Happy mouth, happy can.

Then there was the steroid scandal at the Pan American Games in Caracas, August 1983. A new test showed that many of the athletes were taking steroids to improve their performances. Even Canadians! Now, think back, weren't you secretly proud that our athletes were sleazing around like that? Put us up there with the bad boys. Like the time Margaret Trudeau ran off with the Rolling Stones. All right, Canada!

By the way, this song, available for your listening and dancing pleasure on *What Should I Wear to the Revolution?*, is written in mock Venezuelan style and, trust me, "finish" does rhyme with "spinach" if you use a stage Spanish accent. Gracias.

Scandal in Caracas

In Caracas, Venezuela, there's a scandal
    in the air,
In Caracas, Venezuela, every athlete
    says a prayer:
"Please don't let them take a sample,
Don't let me be an example,"
In Caracas, Venezuela, there's a scandal
    in the air.

At the Pan American games all the heavies
    are competing,
And suddenly there's a new machine
    shows some of them are cheating,
Popping pills to make them bigger,
Ruining their health and figger,
In Caracas, Venezuela, there's a scandal
    in the air.

Everyone knows it happens, it must be
    a Commie plot,
Keeping up with the Soviets, and the crime
    is getting caught,
People admire the athlete, the strength of
    his thighs and fists,
But everyone knows the contest is
    between the scientists.

Caracas, Venezuela, seems like such a
    peaceful place,
With Cubans and Americans united
    in disgrace,
See them trying *not* to win,
Brothers underneath the skin,
In Caracas, Venezuela, even Canada
    loses face.

In Caracas, Venezuela, there's a scandal
    in the air,
In Caracas, Venezuela, all the machos
    must beware,
"With the drugs they have to finish,
All that's left to them is spinach,"
In Caracas, Venezuela, there's a scandal
    in the air.

"Please don't let them take a sample."

Photo: Trish Wilde

There is a B.C.-made feature film of questionable taste called *Big Meat Eater*, and its title kept running through my head when I read the stories on John Turner that came out after he won the Liberal leadership and became, for one brief protein-enriched period, our prime minister.

Mr. Turner was portrayed as a super manly man. He has a steak at least once a day. He likes to hang out with the old boys. He greets everyone with a vigorous handshake. (This was before we found out he was even more tactile than that!)

I was heartbroken when Turner lost power because I loved singing this song. Doug Wilde collaborated on the tune and honest to God, it's the most stirring thing. Please imagine tympanies when you read the lyric.

Boystown-on-the-Rideau

The days of philosophy and flower power
    are gone.
We've got a P.M. we didn't elect and
    his name is John!
He's no square, he's hep, without a flaw,
And there'll be some changes made
    in Ottawa.

Now it's Boystown,
    Boystown-on-the-Rideau.
John and the boys gonna oil
    the big machine;
Bring back the jitterbug and jive,
Put Astroturf in Sussex Drive,
In Boystown-on-the-Rideau,
    know what I mean?

Let me shake your hand, let me
    grab your arm,
Let me wear you down with my
    blue-eyed charm,
Have a steak and a salad, have a
    steak and fries,
Make a couple of calls to a hundred guys.

In Boystown, Boystown-on-the-Rideau,
John and the boys and the
    masculine cuisine;
Steak in peacetime, steak in war,
Makes you bullish at the core,
In Boystown-on-the-Rideau,
    know what I mean?

When duty calls, you give and give,
You gotta be the chief executive,
Gotta wrestle with the balance sheet,
Tell the farmers to get out there
    and raise that cow!
So me and the boys can eat!

In Boystown, Boystown-on-the-Rideau,
John and the boys ain't got no trampoline,
No more joking, no more playing,
Right wing, left wing, he ain't saying,
In Boystown-on-the-Rideau,
Vagueness is the credo,
Boystown-on-the-Rideau.
Boystown.

In August 1983, New York Yankees outfielder Dave Winfield became very famous in Toronto. During a Yankees–Blue Jays game, Mr. Winfield beaned a seagull with a baseball. Bye Bye Birdie, as has been said before.

Then the good part started. Toronto police laid charges against Dave Winfield! Ontario! Is there any place you'd rather be???

Higher authorities were embarrassed by all this and the charges were dropped the next day. The press had fun with it. The *Toronto Sun* ran a picture of the feathered corpse (which was actually taken to Guelph for an autopsy) under the headline "FOUL BALL."

At "Sunday Morning" we, in the words of former producer David McCormick, "kissed it off with a song."

Fly Birdie Fly

He was only a poor wee birdie,
An orphan who had no name,
He was out for the evening
And decided to catch the game,
It was the Yankees against the Blue Jays
And that bird was a proud Canuck,
But when he saw Dave Winfield's
   mighty arm,
He knew he'd run out of luck.

CHORUS:
Fly, birdie, fly
Don't let the Yankees get you,
You survived the acid rain
To die with a baseball in your brain,
Fly, birdie.

He was only a poor wee birdie,
And now he lies in his birdie grave,
But in Toronto we thirst for justice,
And the cops threw the book at Dave,
Because the fans had watched in horror
As the deadly sphere was tossed,
Straight to the mark, like a Cruise
   in the dark,
And the seagull paid the cost.

Then they called the crown attorney,
Because they felt they'd gone astray,
And he looked a touch embarrassed
As he dropped the charge next day,
And the brave arresting officer,
I hear he's dying of shame,
And they'll bury him deep with
   hardly a peep
With the seagull who had no name.

Oh oh, another John Turner song. This one was about his personal housing crisis. He had sold his home in Toronto and was living in House Speaker John Bosley's house until Stornoway, the official residence of the leader of the opposition, could be made liveable. This would cost about half a million dollars to accomplish. The Turners had to have a renovated kitchen and a special cupboard for their silver and, well, it seems when Mulroney was living there he had put in little sinks for his children and they had to be raised because Turner has older kids. You can imagine the pain of it all.

The Bosleys wanted to move into their house, so in April 1985, the Liberal's golden boy had to pack his little bag and move to the Holiday Inn. Sordido!

Homeless Johnny

Oh weep for homeless Johnny,
Oh cry for landless Geills,[1]
It's hard to keep your standards up
When you're leaving Forest Hill,
They've got the looks and the power,
But frankly, what's the point?
Life just ain't worth living
If you can't live in a classy joint.

You can't keep an acre of steak
   in a pokey kitchen
   ("acres of steak, acres of steak"),
And you can't put the silver on a shelf
   from Canadian Tire,
The public's screaming "waste"
But a guy can't live with Tory taste,
And Stornoway is no one's heart's desire.

So weep for homeless Johnny,
Whose life was once so sweet,
He's gonna come back home to Bosley's
And find his files out on the street,
He'll check into hotels, and
all his life he's bound to roam,
Cause it takes a half a million
to make his house a home.

1. Pronounced "Jill."

60

To my mind, stories of political compromise are often the most delicious of all. Prime Minister Mulroney is a man of compromise himself, and he seems to be able to woo others to this philosophy.

In January 1986, the nation was a bit startled to learn that Canada's new ambassador to the republic of Ireland was to be Dennis McDermott, who had just retired as head of the Canadian Labor Congress.

The idea of this outspoken NDP supporter as a diplomat working for the Tory government was a delight and it moved me to write this song. Well, if yuz wants the real truth, Douglas O'Wilde had recently acquired an Irish drum and we were dying to use it in the studio. At any rate, here 'tis.

Oh Dennis

Oh, Dennis is off to Ireland
To do his duty there,
He'll go to cocktail parties
And get out of Mulroney's hair,
And many's the eyebrow raising up
But Dennis he doesn't care,
Dennis is off to Ireland in the morning.

Oh, Dennis is off to Ireland
To be a diplomat,
And all the folks in rank and file
Are tipping him their hat,
They love to see a tiger
Turn into a pussy cat
Dennis is off to Ireland in the morning.

Now every man can be made to bow
And Dennis's price is ninety thou,
A decent wage for working for the Tories,
He'll bite his tongue and pass the test
And put his union past to rest,
Dreaming of the battles and the glories.

Oh, Dennis is off to Ireland
To dwell in marble halls,
He's sure to help the Irish folk
In breaking up their brawls,
It won't be long before he has
Mrs. Thatcher by the throat,
Dennis is off to Ireland in the morning.

All the years with the CLC
He longed to be "your excellency"
And hit the finest parties in the land,
And there's Mulroney in a bind,
There's no more Tories he can find
To take the many honours
That he has at his command.

Oh, Dennis is off to Ireland
And finally it is clear
Just why he's been so quietlike
All through the Tory year,
Sure it's a lovely cap upon
A curious career,
Dennis is off to Ireland in the morning.

(Sure and I smell a manly scent from Canada.)

From Australia came the amazing story of the frozen embryos. I've been singing this song for quite a while now and just can't find an efficient way to tell the convoluted story. Let me try once again.

There is an *in vitro* clinic in the Queen Victoria Medical Centre in Melbourne. And to this clinic came Mario and Elsa Rios, trying to, um, make a baby.

What the doctors do is cut open the woman and remove several eggs. Then they get an anonymous donor to, um, make a donation of sperm. (Rick Whitelaw, my guitarist, assures me, "they don't cut HIM." It figures. Right, my sisters?)

The Rioses, like most of us, weren't quite ready to have their baby, so they left the fertilized eggs in the hospital fridge and flew back to America, and were killed in a plane crash.

Not only was this tragic, but it left the clinic with the sensitive question of what to do with the frozen eggs! Legal issues were raised, especially since the Rioses had money. Presumably the eggs, if implanted and brought to term, would eventually inherit a lot of cash. So, many women volunteered to have the implant. *Even though* doctors pointed out that the fertilization had occurred before the technique was perfected and the eggs might have gone bad.

(I have visions of them dropping each egg in a cup of water. Remember ladies, if it sinks it's fine, if it floats, dump it, right? Thank you, Heloise.)

Australian lawmakers first ruled that the embryos should be thrown away, but that decision was overturned and the last I heard, the upper house of the Victoria state parliament had recommended the embryos be adopted.

In this song, I play the role of one of the eggs. A modest part, but I've made it my own, if I do say so.

Tiny Embryos

*"If somebody cleaned the fridge,
the world would be upset."*

We are frozen embryos from
  down Australia way,
All we want's a little womb where
  we can grow and play,
Mommy's dead, and Daddy didn't leave
  a calling card,
We're still in a test tube and already
  life is hard.

CHORUS:
Life is hard, life is hard
When you can't go out in the yard.

We are frozen embryos, have pity
  on our case,
We ain't got no arms and legs,
  we ain't got no face,
But if somebody cleaned the fridge,
  the world would be upset,
Cause we've got ourselves a lawyer,
  and we're not implanted yet.

Some say the world is full of babies
Who ain't got enough to eat,
Homeless, tiny orphans
With no shoes upon their tiny feet;
So the attention paid to us
May seem a little funny,
If you think so, you're forgetting:
We come from money!
(Our genes would surely be Calvin's!)

We are frozen embryos,
  looking for a mom,
As long as she has lots of dough,
  we don't care where she's from,
We're in legal limbo, so we pray
  we get our wish,
Or stay forever underage, curled up
  in our dish.

CHORUS:
Life is hard, life is hard
When you can't go out in the yard.

Some people don't like this next song. It's the only "Sunday Morning" song not about the Pope that got a lot of negative mail. If you are a compassionate person without a sense of black humour, you may find it creepy; if so, please don't write to me. I *know* what the problems are already. But I decided to include it because it's one of my favourites and it just may cheer up anyone out there who despairs of finding Mr. or Ms. Right.

It's about John Hinckley Junior's new romance.

The news came out in the fall of 1985 that Hinckley, who tried to assassinate President Reagan to impress Jodie Foster, had fallen in love with another patient in the Washington mental hospital where they're both being treated.

NBC reported rumours of a wedding for these two kids.

The woman was an ex-social worker named Leslie DeVeau, who had killed her 10-year-old daughter and blown off her own arm.

"Talk about compatability!" I thought.

Hence – a love song for John and Leslie.

Be My Love or Else

He was the most famous would-be
   assassin in the good old U.S.A.
She was just a humble one-armed
   child killer with a shy and winsome way,
But he looked on her and he knew at once
   'twas she he most adored,
And he said, "Oh, be my darling,
   you're the flower of the ward."

(He said) Be my love – or else
I'll do something I'll regret later,
Be my love – or else
I could be your terminator,
I'm a famous man of action and
   I will not be denied,
Be my love, have my baby, be my bride."

They liked to walk around the grounds
   on a Sunday afternoon,
And they traded medication
   when there was a fullish moon,
And she said "I don't want children much,"
He said "I think I know,
But I've a mind to have a son and
   I'm calling him 'Rambo'."

Be my love – or else
I'll do something I'll regret later,
Be my love – or else
I could be your terminator,
I'm a famous man of action and
   I will not be denied,
Be my love, have my baby, be my bride.

John and Leslie – a match that's
   made in heaven,
John and Leslie – there's so much
   that they share,
Now she has something he ain't got,
She's a somewhat better shot,
But a psychopath in love, he may not care.

(He just says) Be my love – or else
I'll do something I'll regret later,
Be my love – or else
I could be your terminator,
I'm so glad you finally found me,
Wrap your lovin' arm around me,
Jodie couldn't touch you if she tried,
Be my love, have my baby, be my bride.

(And after we're married, we'll write a
book about our lives. And with the
money we make from "Donahue" and
"Merv" and the rights to the pay TV
movie, we can buy our way out of here,
get a little place of our own, with our
very own rifle range. Come fly with
me. . . .)

Religion

This is a short section, because anyone with any brains is not going to write many songs on religious topics. They invite nasty mail from people with too much spare time.

However, once in a while, it just can't be avoided.

The first song was written not for "Sunday Morning" but for CBC TV's New Year's Eve public affairs special in 1980. For several years I was a topical Guy Lombardo summing up the year's events in the fastest, word-heaviest songs I'd ever written.

(One year the show was live with a celebrity studio audience. I had written a patter song ("Karen Kain, acid rain") full of names and events and I just couldn't memorize it in the short time I had. I stuffed the lyrics down my dress as insurance and sure enough, on the second verse I dried. I whipped out the words and gamely carried on.

Many people thought it was part of the act but the pros weren't fooled. Tedde Moore, the actress, later offered me her sympathy.

"They should never have made you sing that *terrible* song," she said.

(I'll say!)

But "Born Again" was easy to learn and I sang it for years. It's about television evangelism and cults. ("Huntley Street" is a reference to the popular Canadian religious talk show "100 Huntley Street," and I guess none of us will ever forget what happened at Jonestown.)

Born Again

Hallelujah, we're all born again,
Turn the TV on and say "amen"
All those friends of Jesus are so
   cheery and sincere,
With the blessings of our wallets,
   they'll hit prime time next year.

There's a revival in religion and
   they're marching to the beat,
It hides away in the Jonestowns and
   shouts on Huntley Street.

At St. Joseph's Oratory,[1]
   they're really doing well,
Three popes in one decade means
   so many things to sell,
The world is going hungry,
   but these holy men still call:
"Have kids! have kids! have kids!"
   till there is no room left at all.

There's a revival in religion and
   I'll tell you how I know:
I called the Ayatollah,
   the Ayatollah tole' me so.

Everybody's searching, my home life
   is a mess,
My oldest boy has shaved his head and
   wears an orange dress,
My daughter is a Moonie, she sits staring
   into space,
And me I pop a Valium for the
   divinest grace.

There's a revival in religion but
   they haven't got me yet,
Though I do admit I cross myself
   when I pass my TV set.
P.T.L.
Pass The Loot.

---

1. St. Joseph's Oratory is an immense tourist attraction in Montreal. It's filled with the crutches of cured pilgrims, and it has a nice little souvenir shop. In my family we remember it vividly because I threw a tantrum there as a child and refused to go in. It was my brothers' fault, okay?

At the risk of being thought obsessed, I'm including two songs about Pope John Paul II.

But when you're raised Presbyterian in a small town you can't help being fascinated by everything about the Catholic Church.

In my town, the population was 50-50 Protestant-Catholic. We went to separate schools, hung around different restaurants, and were told dreadful things about each other by our religious leaders. If a Catholic kid spent an evening at the YMCA, he had to tell about it in confession the following Saturday.

And if one of Ours married one of Theirs, the big question was always "did he 'turn' or did she?"

"The priest comes to your house and talks you into 'turning'. He makes you sign a paper and when you have children they come and get them and send them straight to Rome," we were told.

"We talk directly to God, they have to deal with his mom. Tsk tsk."

Meanwhile, the Catholic kids were being informed that we were doomed to go immediately to hell, without even a stop in Limbo ("how low can you go?").

Of course the most fascinating Catholic of all has got to be the Pope himself.

As a feminist, I have mixed feelings about the man. I admire him for his language skills, his TV savvy, his athletic prowess, his sense of fashion (as *Glamour* magazine used to advise, "find your look and stick to it"), and his literary skills. It seems this guy can do anything. He even has an album that's a slow but steady seller at Sam the Record Man's.

But let's face it, with his ultra-conservative views on birth control and the role of women in the world, he's caused a lot of heartache and social problems.

I put some of these thoughts into this song in August 1982.

Papal Bull

I'm glad I'm not a Catholic when
    I listen to the Pope,
He speaks a zillion languages but
    he comes off like a dope,
His attitude to women is
    politically incorrect,
But from a celibate in a long white dress,
    what can we expect?

He wants to keep us pregnant and
    three steps behind our men,
He wants to bring the middle ages
    rolling back again,
He wants me in a welfare line with
    seven kids in tow,
If I didn't have such respect for him
    I'd tell him where to go.

My tendency is to laugh at him,
But like the French,
    I'm "laughing yellow,"[1]
Cause we're not talking local crazies here,
This is one influential fellow.

I wish I'd been in England when
    His Holiness was on tour,
And they sold papal souvenirs because
    the Vatican is so poor,
The Pope was on the T-shirts,
    the watches and the spoons,
The keys of old St. Peter's on
    the helium balloons.

I'm glad I'm not the Vatican nun who
    does his laundry every night,
I'm sure she says "Please, father,
    for travel, not the white!"
And when he kisses tarmacs she prays
    "God, protect each cuff"
I hear life in the papal laundry
    is a penance very tough.

You may think that this is just
    a feminist complaint,
And you may think His Holiness is
    one step short of saint,
Yes, I confess I'm jealous,
    though I'd never want to be a priest,
I just hate to see his album sell when
    I can't get mine released.[2]   Amen.

---

1. "Rire jaune" – I've always figured the English equivalent was the Damon Runyon expression "castor oil smile." My dictionary says it means "to laugh on the wrong side of the mouth."

2. I wasn't able to find a record company interested in releasing *Unexpected*. Eventually I started my own company (the grasping conglomerate "Mouton Records"), and released the album myself. It's not quite the same thing. I don't know who signed the Pope to record his Polish folk song LP, but I do know that the day the assassination attempt was made on him, a famous Toronto record store front-racked J.P. II's disc.

Nancy's alter ego, Fiona Freud, Second Lady of the Guitar, goes through an arduous recording session with her producer Johnny Ladron.

Then in 1984 it was announced that the Pope was going to pay a visit to Canada. Canada!! The Boy Scout of nations. We couldn't figure out why. I mean, the Pope had been travelling to the war zones, to areas of conflict like Central America and Poland.

I figured he knew that in the fall of 1984 something appalling would happen in Canada and we'd want to turn to him for consolation.

Sure enough, in September, the federal Tories swept the polls!

I had hoped the Pope's visit here would bring a flood of tacky souvenirs, as they'd had in England, but it was not to be. So the reference to "Papal Pampers" for busy moms was a bit premature on my part.

The two towns mentioned in the last verse, Midland and Downsview, were the places where the Pope was to say mass in Ontario. I thought they were perfect names, like "Anywhere, U.S.A.," the ideal places to search for the Canadian soul.

Kiss Our Tarmac

Oh he only comes to troubled places,
To console the ones who're in
  the most distress,
He likes to put a smile on hopeless faces,
Guess he's heard that Canada's a mess.
Is he coming to heal a house divided?
Is he coming to save the baby seals?
Or do we have lefty priests
  who must be chided?[1]
Wonder what the Papa's thinking
  as he kneels?

So kiss our tarmac, Holy Father,
Raise your saintly eyes above,
Tell us battling French and English
All we really need is love
Send us women to the kitchen,
We can raise some babies there,
And we'll buy some Papal Pampers
To remind us that you care.

Oh he seems to like to hit the hot spots
Where there's tanks in the street,
  and guerillas in the hills,
In Canada where will he aim his
  Papal pot shots?
There's just lotteries and
  contraceptive pills.

So come to Midland! Come to Downsview,
Looking for our country's soul,
We will touch you with our faith and love
And super crowd-control,
Those little buildings that we're putting up,
We'll name them after you
A million Johnny-Paulies-on-the-Spot,
It's the least that we can do.
    May God bless you,
    Bienvenue.

---

1. This is a reference to Father Ernesto Cardinal, Nicaragua's minister of culture. I'm sure we all remember the news shot of the Pope shaking his finger in Cardinal's face during the Papal visit to Managua.

Nancy as a Girl Guide, probably in 1960. "The admonition 'a Guide smiles and sings under all difficulties' has stood me in good stead when I've had to write cheery little songs about Tories."

Playing Katisha in a Dalhousie University production of The Mikado, 1966. "This was the highlight of my showbiz career. It's been downhill ever since."

First professional show — a Young People's Theatre tour of Under Milkwood in Toronto. That's Nancy under the lamp; others in the cast were, from left, Ian McLeish, Irene Hogan, Peter Blais, Tim Leary, and Beth Kaplan, all of whom would probably prefer this photo not be published.

Publicity shot, about 1974.

Fiona Freud serenades a bunch of guys. From the postcard series "Fiona Freud, Guys and Tomatoes."

At the Jasper Folk Festival, August 1985.

Photo: Larry LeBlanc

Photo: Trish Wilde

According to a *Globe and Mail* story, there are about one hundred Jehovah's Witnesses in Alberta who believe that Michael Jackson is Jesus Christ.

Not that Michael is a friend of Jesus, or even a cousin. He *is* Jesus.

These people have lots of proof. They point to the singer's pure life, his gifts to charity, and the miracle of his hair going on fire during his Pepsi commercial. And, well, look at the facts. Both his names have seven letters, just like Jehovah or Messiah.

Sounds logical to me. So I wrote them this hymn.

Blessed Michael Hear Our Hymn of Joy

Blessed Michael, hear our hymn of joy,
We believe you are the holy boy,
You must be God, because you sing
   so good,
Thy kingdom come today in Hollywood.

Blessed Michael, hear our hymn of praise,
How we rejoiced to see your hair ablaze,
Your miraculous survival was
   a sign from above,
Blessed Michael, please accept our love.

Every command we obey from you,
You say to "beat it!", so rest assured *we* do,
The light beneath your footsteps is
   our beacon bright,
We'll follow you like children through
   the "Thriller" night.

Hear us, oh Michael, as we rhapsodize,
We've heard you say you're
   "not like other guys,"
Grant us a benediction from
   your sacred glove,
And we'll believe that Billie Jean
   is not your love.

Out here in Alberta we're a lonely crew,
We must meet in secret just to
   worship you,
Heathen people here say you're no deity,
Please forgive them, they believe
   in Wayne Gretzky.[1]

Amen, amen, aaaaaaaaaaaaaaaa-men.

1. So do I.

It's Outrageous

The songs inspired by outrageous stories turn out to be mainly about political events, so I thought I'd arrange them in chronological order. Hey, I know you're thinking, what a brilliant, original idea. The woman is clearly a genius; possibly a national treasure. Yes, I guess it's true.

Actually, the first song is not even a song – it's a mock poem. I can't do real poetry because I don't much like it (ooops, terrible admission). But this is a work in the pretentious-poetry-for-pretentious-reading vein, and it's about an outrageous place, an outrageous souvenir, and the outrageous behaviour of the RCMP that came to light in the late seventies. I wrote this, whatever it is, in September 1981.

Mountie-in-the-Snow

Oh joy, oh rapture, oh Niagara Falls,
Just two feet away from the
   Harry Houdini Museum
(Jeez, Madge, didn't know
   Harry was Canadian)
The souvenir shop to end all
   souvenir shops,
And there, oh joy, oh rapture,
The souvenir to end all souvenirs.
Oh god, my darling, my coveted,
   my most lusted-after
Mountie-in-the-Snow.
Hey, all you English majors,
fourteen lines and never yet a verb,
   ain't poetry
A treat!
Mountie-in-the-Snow, what a saucy fellow,
Mountie-in-the-Snow, with his stripes
   of yellow,[1]
(But stop, stop! I of all people do not
   believe in the parody form.)
Mountie-in-the-Snow,
So stern and calm, even as de flakes fly
   in de face,

So tiny, yet so tall,
Never a flicker of emotion.
Ice blue eyes.
Scarlet tanager tunic.
Black b-b-b-b-boots – hubba hubba.
What cares he for the
   McDonald Commission?[2]
What does HE know of the burning
   of barns and the
steam kettle at the flap of the envelope?
All he knows is, just a few more feet
And he might make Musical Ride.
Mountie-in-the-Snow!
I want him so bad I can taste him,
But I turn away,
Heartbroken,
My bulging wallet intact.
For he is "made in Taiwan"
And I am a cultural nationalist.
Oh woe, oh woe,
He set my heart aglow,
though,
Mountie-in-the-Snow.

---

1. These lines are sung to the tune of "Robin in the Rain."

2. The McDonald Commission was set up in 1977 to investigate stories of "RCMP wrongdoing." Many of these turned out to be true and often had taken place in Quebec in an attempt to thwart separatist efforts to make the province an independent country. Mounties, it turns out, had burned down a barn and broken into an office. They had steamed open mail and generally behaved in quite a high-handed way.

In introducing this next song (from December 1981) I often asked the audience what institutions they hated most. Turns out they hated a lot of things, the federal government, Bell Canada, even CBC (WHAT???), but we usually agreed the most arrogant organization we have to deal with in our daily lives is the bank.

I eventually stopped singing the song because certain things, like 24% interest, had changed. But in many respects it's getting worse. Large charges for services, low interest on savings, huge lineups, bad treatment of employees – the list goes on and on. Stephen Leacock was right.

(This song was written for one of the CBC TV year-end specials I've already mentioned.)

We're the Banks

All across the nation, we hear the cries
  of pain,
The people watch their savings going
  clockwise down the drain,
The farmers lose their acreage,
  the plants are closing fast,
And little stores have just a few
  more months that they can last,
The jobless rate goes climbing,
  the interest rate the same,
Receiverships and bankruptcies are
  just a daily game,
Consumers use the plastic,
  but they'd better pay on time,
Cause interest set at 24 percent is not
  a crime,
But we pay no attention to the fuss,
Cause everybody's hurting but us.

We are the Royal Bank of Canada,
  the T.D. and the Montreal,
The Scotia and the Commerce,
  and you know we're going to
  screw you all,
You need us, but you hate us,
Cause they can't regulate us,
You know it was ever thus,
Everybody's hurting but us.

We make you stand in line-ups,
  we wear your patience thin,
Sometimes we even charge you to
  put your money in,
We lend at higher interest than
  we'd ever pay to you,
So we can build high towers with
  a panoramic view,
The profits that we make are scandalous,
And everybody's hurting but us.

(Continues overleaf)

We are the Commerce and the Scotia and
  the Royal Bank of Canada,[1]
And we take your tiny dollars and
  we lend them to South Africa,
And you're naive and silly
To protest our loans to Chile,
That junta's so industrious!
And everybody's hurting but us.

Did you ever wonder what happened to
  Mary-of-the-Royal? ("Hi, I'm Mary.")[2]
Mary was a pretty girl, but
  Mary wasn't very loyal,
    ("Say, where *is* Mary?")
We let her go because we heard that she
  was trying to join a union,
  such a disgrace,
The banks like girls who never
  forget their place
  (on their feet, at the counter,
  and smiling.)

We hire the nicest women to do
  our dirty work,
So anybody who complains will feel
  like such a jerk,
Our mortgage rates are out of sight,
  you can't afford to pay,
And guess who'll be the one who comes to
  take your home away!
Anne Murray thinks we're marvellous,[3]
And everybody's hurting but us.

But we never forget to say "thanks –
  have a nice day,"
We're the banks.

1. I purposely left the Toronto Dominion Bank off this guilt list, because they had bowed to pressure and no longer invested in South Africa.

2. "Mary-of-the-Royal" was a character who appeared for several years in a particularly irritating series of Royal Bank TV commercials. She played a super friendly, super helpful teller.

3. Canada's most famous singer was spokesperson in the Bank of Commerce commercials for several years.

In Canada we have two types of lottery, the better-chance-of-being-struck-by-lightning kind for most of us poor schmucks, and the special kind for the privileged and politically astute. This latter lottery is called Getting Appointed to the Senate. And just before Prime Minister Pierre Trudeau (see chapter on "Royalty") resigned, he passed out senatorships with a generous, Liberal hand.

Fortunately for me, the tradition of patronage continued under the Tories, so this song remains ever green. Merci, Brian.

He Smiled on You

Oh yes it must feel wonderful,
Oh yes, it must feel fine,
Your phone rings in the morning –
It's the P.M. on the line!
He says "I want to pay you back
For all you've done for me,
Come up to Ottawa, my dear,
and work for democracy."

HALLELUJAH! You're in the senate now,
You played your cards right,
    now you're a sacred cow,
So bring a can of Brasso for the
    plaque on your door,
'Cause you ain't gonna work no more. NO!
    You ain't gonna work no more!

In a country with no classes
You're the aristocracy,
Enjoy your discount haircuts
And your hefty salary,
You may be a failed candidate
or just a backroom boy,
But up in Ottawa, my dear,
They'll keep you from the hoi polloi.

HALLELUJAH! you can't believe it's true,
You're in the senate, The Man
    has smiled on you,
Now everyone appreciates what
    your brown nose is for,
Cause you ain't gonna work no more,
No, you ain't gonna work no more.

HALLELUJAH! You got a senate seat!
You won the lottery, now you're the
    new elite,
And you'll be laughing last when they call
    you "dinosaur,"
Cause you ain't gonna work no more,
No, you ain't gonna work no more.
It's the Canadian dream.

"Fluffy, you're a regular stinko."

I'm not automatically drawn to the business section when I settle down with a newspaper, but in April 1984, that section carried a wonderful story about INCO's annual shareholders' meeting.

INCO is the big nickel mining company in Sudbury, Ontario, which cleaned up the town's pollution problem by building a 1,250 foot smoke stack. Now emissions from the plant go all over Ontario, possibly even into the United States. But Sudbury's okay.

Over the years there's been a lot of pressure on INCO to reduce the emissions of sulfur dioxide. Currently they've got it down to a refreshing 1,950 tons *a day*.

At this particular shareholders' meeting, participants included a man who wanted INCO to reimburse him for his hair loss, which he claimed was their fault, and an environmentalist dressed up as a dead fish.

But INCO's chairman Charles Baird was a match for all the bleeding hearts. He said there is "no proof" that INCO is responsible for acid rain.

Hey, Mr. Baird, go get 'em!

(Author's note: In the reference to my cat, I changed her name to "Fluffy" to protect her. Her real name is Pizzicatto. I know. Groan. But I am trying to tell the truth here. Like Mr. Baird.)

Don't Blame INCO

Blame it on the Yanks,
Blame it on the banks,
Blame it on some communist pranks,
But don't blame INCO!

If you gotta complain
About the acid rain,
You can talk about the pain,
But don't blame INCO.

'Cause there's "no proof"
   there's any connection
Between rusty cars and
   Sudbury wind direction,
No proof that sulfur dioxide is bad for you,
And our buddies at Queen's Park
   don't mind a dead fish
   or two.

Confidence restored
By the chairman of the board,
I feel a little floored,
But I don't blame INCO.

(A Poem – to C.B.)
It often happens
My cat comes in;
She smells like a can
That's made of tin.
I say "Fluffy,
you're a regular stinko,
But God forbid
I should blame this on INCO."

It's dirty on the shore,
Our eyes are red and sore,
But we'll study it some more,
And we won't blame INCO.

Whitehorse was the worst.

I've played all over Canada, but Whitehorse was the worst.

It was a wonderful town to sing in, and the event, a folk festival in February, was quite exciting. And it's a spectacularly beautiful place.

But almost everyone I met in my three days there had to tell me, unasked, his or her opinion of Toronto.

They all hate it. They all felt compelled to tell me why they lived in Whitehorse instead of Toronto.

Had I asked? Did I particularly care?

No.

It never seems to occur to people that by going on and on about how obnoxious Toronto is (it isn't, by the way), they are insulting my personal taste. After all, Toronto is the place I've chosen to live in. These same people would never say "My god, that's an ugly dress you're wearing," but they might as well.

So when, in the fall of 1985, a new environmental study showed that the Great Lakes Basin, which has Toronto in it, is one of the most toxic areas in the world, that those of us who live here already have 20 percent more toxic substances in our systems than do people in other parts of the country, I thought at once of all those folks across this mighty land who hate us.

"How happy they must be today," I thought, "especially in Whitehorse!"

This song was my attempt to find a silver lining in a rather depressing cloud.

Happy Now?

From coast to coast there sounds a cheer,
They've got the news they longed to hear,
The city they all love to hate
Is suffering a cruel fate,
The Great Lakes Basin's had the biz,
And that is where Toronto is,
Our food is poisoned, so's our air,
Guess there's rejoicing everywhere.

Are you happy on the Prairies tonight?
Is it almost like a dream come true
To know that the livers of Hogtown are
    full of PCBs,
And those Bloor Street sophisticates all
    wish they were you?
Are you delirious down Nova Scotia way,
Do you put down your flagons and say
"All our life we've been jealous
Of Toronto gals and fellows,
Now they're poisoned, so hip hip hooray."

(spoken section)
(You know, folks, someone once said that
    Toronto had no heart,
That all we ever cared about was being
    beautiful and smart,
We thought a PCB was a second-rate Tory,
Now we're doomed, and you've
    always put us down,
But I bet you won't say you're sorry.)

Are you enchanté in old Montreal?
Can you scarcely suppress a glad cry
Until you remember with tearful recall
All the Montrealers who came here to die?
Are you thrilled in the north and B.C.
That we're building up immunity?
While we cough here in the dark
The joggers smile in Stanley Park
    (Actually, if I had to choose between
        dioxins on my plate and Bill Bennett in
        my legislature, I think I'd stay put.)
Are you happy all over Canada? Oui oui?

I don't often write about U.S. politics because it baffles me. I mean, their senators are so young. What's going on down there?

But in May 1984, I wrote a little number expressing that very bafflement. It was about Ron and Nancy Reagan's goodwill trip to China.

I don't want to start an ugly rumour, but I have it on good authority that China is a "communist" country. Much more communist than Nicaragua, for instance. But instead of sending contras in and mining the harbors of Chinese ports, Ron and Nancy went over and had a lovely social time.

I repeat. What *is* going on in Amurrica?

Nancy with producer-bongoista Matt Zimbel at recording session for Unexpected.

Nancy and Ronnie in China

I read the papers, I'm scratching my head,
Well you know what I mean-oh,
Is it just news, or is it some weird
  propaganda?
When Nancy and Ronnie put mines
  in the harbour of Puerto Sandino,
Then fly off to China to rescue
  the Communist panda.

You've got to choose your
  commie friends with care,
Go to those with bucks to spare,
When talk of trade is in the air
  it's okay if they're godless heathens,
Peking good, Managua bad,
Sandinistas make us mad,
Their revolution's just a fad,
  and we don't believe they're Catholics.

Now is it hypocrisy? Is it diplomacy?
Was it a dream?
Did President Reagan really
  shake hands with a red?
Is Nancy a contra who went there resolved
  to destroy the regime?
But they don't get attacked,
  they get nuclear power instead?

(Nancy's diary): "Dear Diary,
the Great Wall's enormous,
  it took my breath away,
But I nearly lost my breakfast
  at the acupuncture display.
I like to be the president's wife,
  you see what the tourists don't see,
And I liked Deng Xiaoping,
  and Deng Xiaoping liked me."

They censored his speech,
  but he didn't complain,
After all, when in Rome,
That Ronnie's an affable fellow,
  we all must agree,
And as long as the part about Russia
  got through to the people back home,
He got the votes in the Peking primary.

At a Toronto peace rally, October 1983, with Marie Lynn Hammond.

Ever since International Women's Year, 1975, we gals have been busy assessing our social and political progress.

In May 1984, there was a juxtaposition of events in Canada that lead me to feel it's been two steps forward, four steps back.

First the good news. Madame Jeanne Sauvé was sworn in as our first woman governor general.

The same week a woman prison guard in Northern Ontario told the press that part of her job was to buy *Playboy* and *Penthouse* for the inmates.

Gilles Gregoire, released from jail after serving a sentence on a conviction of sexually molesting young girls, insisted on taking back his seat in the Quebec National Assembly.

And in Alberta, Woodward's, the family department store, discovered that a fast seller for them was a novelty item: foam rubber baseball bats with the words "child beater" or "wife beater" inscribed thereon.

Herewith, a musical progress report.

Bats for Brats

A woman for governor general!
That's a social gain, I suppose.
But I look at the rest of the news and I say
"Plus ça change, plus c'est la même chose."
The very same day that Madame Sauvé
Was proving there's no one eliter,
In Edmonton people bought baseball bats
Inscribed with the words "wife beater."

So shop at Woodward's for the toys
That make the boys
Grow into men
Who now and then
Think it is perfectly okay
To give "the wife" a little clout
Or grab the kids and knock them out
In that amusing manly way;
Yes, buy your brat
A baseball bat
That tells exactly where we're at,
Some people change, but others never will,
No one minds what bones you broke,
To beat your wife is still a joke
In Edmonton just like on Parliament Hill.[1]

Meanwhile, in Quebec City,
    where the fleur-de-lis unfurls,
Monsieur Gilles Gregoire he does okay,
After nine months in the slammer for
    molesting little girls,
He goes back to work as an MNA.

And the lady politicians say
"I'm not a feminist, no way,
I got into politics
'cause it's a great place to meet guys...."

So shop at Woodward's for the kind of toy
That the whole family can enjoy,
And you can quickly prove that
    ugly rumour,
Show it to your better half,
And when you notice she don't laugh, say
"See – women have *no sense of humour*."

---

1. Some of Canada's sensitive MPs laughed heartily when a question about wife beating was asked in the House of Commons a couple of years ago. And in 1985, Dave Nickerson, the MP from Western Arctic (N.W.T.), resumed his seat in the House after being convicted on a charge of assaulting his wife. To their credit, the members booed, but Brian Mulroney refused to suspend him.

John Turner's bum-patting gaffe became so famous so quickly that someone sent me a cartoon on it from a Seattle paper, and a Kitchener – Waterloo women's group designed and wore a protective garment called "The Turner Shield" on "The National" one night.

Mr. Turner was prime minister at the time, and he publicly greeted Liberal party president Iona Campagnola with a hearty pat on the behind. He did it to a Quebec politician as well.

Some people thought it an unseemly gesture.

A lot of women do not enjoy being greeted that way.

Believe me.

Mr. Turner apparently didn't believe the people who told him this, and he explained that he was a warm, tactile kind of guy and it was his style to touch people. He did it again a couple of times and the press had a wonderful time.

Personally I don't think it was such a good career move for Mr. Turner, who soon went down to a disastrous defeat in the fall election.

Cute story, though.

T for Tactile

When you're riding in the Paris subway,
Packed in like sardines,
And you feel a hand on your behind,
You know what that means,
It's get off at the next stop
Or hold your ground and fight,
But it's different in Ottawa, Canada,
It's a Liberal delight.

If you feel a too-familiar pat
That's friendly as can be,
Hold your temper, sister,
You've just met Johnny T.

T for tactile,
Touch you anywhere,
T for "tell your prudish friends,
Frankly, I don't care,
Cause I'm a warm, outgoing person, baby,
I admire your derrière,
And after eight years in the private sector,
    these hands have got a lot to share."

When you're working in the factory,
Standing by the big machines,
And the boss comes up and grabs you
On the seat of your blue jeans,
You can testify at hearings,
Or take your pay and go,
But in loftier social circles
It's the Sussex Drive "hello."

If you feel a too-familiar pat
That's friendly as can be,
Think of your future, sister,
And smile for Johnny T.

T for tacky,
Try not to retreat,
T for take it with a smile
'cause you can stand the heat,
If your ass can take the indignity
It could have the system beat,
It could find itself one day settling into
    a sumptuous senate seat.

When a world-famous hawk turns into a dove overnight, you have to wonder about it. When that hawk is the president of the United States, you wonder even more.

But it doesn't seem to matter what Ronald Reagan does. His popularity continues to soar, and nobody took much notice when he went to the United Nations in September 1984 and started talking peace.

Mr. Sincerity

Ronnie always was a kidder,
Ronnie always loved to tease,
And just before an election, God knows,
Ronnie sure tries to please.
He says "never mind what I said before,
The stuff about the 'winnable nuclear war,'
When I find myself at the big U.N.,
Praise Jesus, I'm a peacenik, born again."

So fly, fly, born-again dove,
Show the Soviets a little brotherly love,
When they look up to watch you fly,
You can let 'em have it in the eye.

Ronnie always spoke of 'the evil empire'
And 'nuclear warning shots',
Now he's quoting Gandhi
And spouting peaceful thoughts.
Hey look! It's Mr. Nice Guy,
He just wants a brand new start,
Well some might say "hypocrisy!",
But I say "change of heart."

So fly, fly, born-again dove,
Show the Soviets a little brotherly love,
When they look up to watch you fly,
You can let 'em have it, you can let 'em
    have it in the eye, let 'em have it
    in the eye.

Mr. Sin – ce – ri – teeeee,
That's what you seem – to – be,
It doesn't matter what you do – or – say,
You've got the heart of the U.S.A.,
You can rape your own land,
    you can starve the poor,
Invade another country, but you
    still endure,
They can catch you in a lie,
    you get off scot free,
Mr. Sin–ce–ri–ty.

So fly, fly, born-again dove,
Show the Soviets a little brotherly love,
When they look up to watch you fly,
You can let 'em have it,
    you can let 'em have it in the
        eye . . . ., let 'em have it in the
        eye . . . ., let 'em have it in the
        eye . . . ., let 'em have it in the eye.

In April 1985, there occurred a great international injustice. Our warrior novelist Farley Mowat was refused admission to the United States.

Farley was enraged. I daresay he still is. We all were. Apparently he was on some sort of "list."

That's what they say. But I think they were just nervous about what he'd do at their parties!

No Farleys

Well, the greatest country in the world
is the good ole U.S.A.;
And everybody in the world
better do what the U.S. say;
We ain't scared of anyone,
the Russians or Chinese,
But there's a certain guy
who brings us trembling to our knees!
So we don't allow no Farleys 'round here.

We don't like Farley Mowat,
and we don't like his friends,
You let in one guy like him
and who knows where it ends,
He says he's here to sell some books,
but he don't give no details,
We know he'll corrupt our youth
and make them save the whales.
So we don't allow no Farleys 'round here.

No Farleys, we're sorry,
    we're not going to back down,
No pinkos, no weirdos,
    it's time for a crackdown,
We don't need our files to establish
    his guilt,
And who can say what he keeps
    under his kilt.
    (Ooh, is that a baby beluga?)

He claims he went to Russia
and found some humans there!
That theory is at odds
with everything that we hold dear,
And Farley's so persuasive
that he poses serious threats
To young Americans like
Son of Sam and Bernard Goetz,
So we don't allow no Farleys 'round here.

We talked to your Mounties cause
    we're not so dumb here,
No mouse-eating, wolf-loving authors
    can come here,
Politically speaking he's way out of tune,
And frankly we're scared he might
    throw us a moon.
We don't allow no Farleys,
No commie-lovin' Charleys,
We don't allow no Farleys around here.

The Tory finance minister Michael Wilson (have you noticed he was never called "boring" after he got that job?) brought down his first budget in May 1985, and it made a lot of people scream.

In fact elderly people screamed so hard about the Tory plan to de-index the old age pension that Wilson and Mulroney had to back down on the whole plan.

Big Shot Budget

It's a big shot budget and
   the big shots smile,
It's a big shot budget in a Bay Street style,
And the minister of finance bought
   new shoes
Now you and I sing the Bay St. blues.
Pain, pain, pain.

There'll be tax on this and tax on that,
Tax for the lean but not for the fat,
And the smokers gag and the drinkers sigh
And a lot of dreams are kissed goodbye.
Pain, pain, pain.

It's big shot budget, all agree,
Good for Business, bad for me,
Time at last for common sense,
A billion more for our defence!

Hear strangled cries from coast to coast
As yuppies learn they'll hurt the most,
Folks with kids, dogs and cats
Must underwrite aristocrats.
Pain, pain, pain.

Goodness no, we won't tax the rich,
But we found a way to make 'em twitch,
Wilson's populist at the core:
They can't write off that yacht no more.
Pain, pain, pain.

It's a big shot budget and I'm so small,
Thank God Mike Duffy explained it all,
He put "jobs-jobs-jobs" in simple terms:
It means more work for accounting firms.
Pain, pain, pain.

Pain, pain, pain (if you drive a car)
Pain, pain, pain (if you're saving for a home)
Pain, pain, pain (if you try to run a farm)
Pain, pain, pain (if you fish the sea)
Pain, pain, pain (if you work in the plant)
Pain, pain, pain (in Port Hawkesbury)
Pain, pain, pain (if you wash your hair)
Pain, pain, pain (if you feed your cat)
Pain, pain, pain . . .

With guitarist Rick Whitelaw (left) and Vancouver pianist Michael Creber at Vancouver East Cultural Centre. Nancy did a week of concerts there in April 1985.

Conductor Boris Brott presents a lovely bouquet to Fiona Freud following her orchestral debut with the Hamilton Philharmonic in November 1985.

These days, when you go to the South Pacific, you don't find Mary Martin and Ezio Pinza.

You find Greenpeace and the French, and they ain't talking "Happy Talk."

The French have been testing nuclear weapons at their Pacific colonies for years, and the Greenpeacers have been trying to harass them into stopping.

In July of 1985, the French government arranged to have the Greenpeace ship *Rainbow Warrior* sunk, and a Dutch photographer on board was killed.

It was quite a scandal, but it didn't seem to touch the French government all that much. At one point the two French spies who bombed the boat were receiving 150 supportive letters a week from French citizens.

When I perform "French from France," I tell the audience that "Sunday Morning" sent me to Mururoa Atoll to raise the morale of French troops and nuclear scientists there. Then I get them to pretend they are at little tables smoking stinking Gitanes and hoisting what a friend of mine once called "a cravate of wine," and they sing along.

We have a lovely time.

French from France

When we set off those bombs in Mururoa,
Nobody's supposed to mind.
We're surprised the Greenpeace
   cuckoo boys
Are treating us so unkind.
For the folks who live along the Seine
Hear a little boom and they say "amen,"
They favour the neutron dance
As long as it's not in France.

What's all the fuss about a tiny little place,
One little Pacific atoll?
So what if it's sinking into the blue sea,
Fifty centimetres, that's all;
We must test the weapons in case
   there's a war,
And that's what a faraway colony's for,
Best place for the double check,
Quel dommage that we lost Quebec!

We're the French from France and
   we blow up the seas
Ooh la la la, c'est si bomb,
We're the French from France and
   we do as we please,
Ooh la la la, c'est si bomb,
When the Russians (Yankees) go testing
   we say it's deplorable,
But we do the same, people think
   "how adorable!"
We can't help our belligerent stance,
We're the French from France.

The tasteless protesters
   (they're stuck in the sixties,)
They'd better stay out of our way,
Don't fool with the country of
   Bardot and Cousteau and
Croissants and cafe au lait,
And the Nouvelle Zealanders
   can bleat in our ear,
When you're setting off bombs it's
   too noisy to hear,
So no more Mr. Gentil Guy,
They can quiche their boats goodbye.

"Dump it in the Third World" is kind of a mean-spirited song, but it does illustrate a phenomenon which I find interesting.

This is it: If I feel really angry about something I can't write about it very well. My irritation gets in the way.

Subject: cigarettes.

All my life, cigarette smokers have made me miserable.

So when I hear Canada's tobacco farmers whining because their sales are down, I find it hard to be objective.

And when I see one hand of the federal government spending $1.1 million on an anti-smoking campaign aimed at teenagers, while the other hand gives $90 million to tobacco farmers so they can store their noxious crop until prices are better, I chuckle, "oh, those Tories!" But my laughter has a hollow ring.

So, this song isn't all that hilarious. I'm sorry, I just have this hang-up.

I also discovered in the course of writing this that I couldn't spell "emphysema." This put me squarely in my place.

Dump It in the Third World

Everyone admires the tobacco farmer,
He works hard by the sweat of his brow,
Growing the poison to choke the world
And he sees himself as a martyr now;
All of them wimps, giving up smoking,
Government telling all the kids to stop,
People got a right to emphysema,
Farmer can't get a fair price for the crop.

So dump it in the third world,
Dump it in the third world,
They love a cigarette between their lips
And we don't have to bother with filter tips
   (down there)
Dump it on the third world.

Shed a tear for the tobacco farmer,
His story's sad and his story's true,
He's too old to learn a new trick,
He don't want to grow something
   that's good for you.
Tobacco farmer's a resourceful person,
He's travelled enough to hear
   the people say:
"Send your tobacco to our poor country,
We want to die the North American way."

Dump it in the third world,
Dump it in the third world,
They love a cigarette between their lips
And we don't have to bother with filter tips
   (down there)
Dump it in the third world.

The farmers get together and
   the air is grey and thick,
One says "we've got a problem and
   together we must stick,
We're fighting for the rights of Canadians
   to make other Canadians sick,
And you know me, boys,
   I'd die for freedom."

Hell, let's dump it in the third world,
Dump it in the third world,
They love a cigarette between their lips,
And we don't have to bother with filter tips,
Dump it in the third world.

Royalty

I feel so cheap when I read about royalty. But I can't help myself. Writing about them is not quite so degrading, for some reason.

The first song I wrote about the royal family (and here I speak of the Windsors of England) was called "Teenage Prince." It was a lovesick song about that cute Prince Andrew who was then studying in Canada at Lakefield College. After the little ingrate turned twenty, I had to cut it from my repertoire, which was a bit of a blow.

Next came a number called "Queensong" in which I had the queen singing to the Scottish nationalists in a Glasgow accent.

And then Lady Diana appeared on the scene.

Wasn't it wonderful? Just when Margaret Trudeau was fading from sight, along came a viable substitute object for our curiosity and worship.

The courtship of Diana and Prince Charles was an exciting time for us all, and surely the best moment came when her uncle or her father (can't remember which) assured the press that she was a virgin. How he knew was a great mystery.

This little song became the title tune for a cabaret show I did. Like many of my hits it had a short life, for Diana was soon married and pregnant. I just can't keep up with these young people, although I'm considering rewriting the song for Brooke Shields.

The Last Virgin on the Planet

His Highness went a hunting
  for the perfect one,
A cross between Bo Derek and
  The Singing Nun,
Someone aristocratic,
  whom he could adore,
But someone whom nobody had
  adored before.

She's the last virgin on the planet,
Her willpower is granite,
She broke the hearts of a dozen males,
Even said no to the Prince of Wales.
She's the last virgin left in London,
She won't let herself be undone,
She stayed away from the frats and woods
'Cause a prince won't settle for
  damaged goods.

She's the last virgin in the U.K.,
See her toss the bridal bouquet,
We don't care if she's a bit too tall,
She hooked the biggest fish of all,
She's the last virgin ever sighted,
We're all delirious and delighted,
A jaded world has something new to try:
Can we wear our hair like Lady Di?

How can we tell that she's still untouched?
Her daddy told us so,
We take it all with a grain of salt,
'Cause Daddy's always the last to know.
  (Does *your* daddy know about *you*)?

She's the last virgin, Lady Di is,
Shows us what demure and shy is,
She set her cap for a certain man,
But she won't ride a horse with
  Princess Anne,
She's the last virgin that we know of,
She's not stuck up or a show-off,
Her thoughts are pure and
  her money's clean,
If Liz steps down, we'll have a
  teenage queen.

Dream on, dream on, Teenage Queen,
Here comes *People* magazine,
You're a girl who sure knows how,
Got yourself a good job now,
Dream on, dream on, Lady Di,
Save it for that special guy,
You're so young and he's so old,
Glad you were so self-controlled,
Lady, lady
  Di–ay–ay–ay–ay–ay
  Di–ay–ay–ay–ay–ay - ay.

In the spring of 1983, Diana and Charles visited Canada. Oh the joy, the excitement. For us, at least. But I felt a little sorry for the royals.

I mean, who plans these tours? If you deliberately set out to bore a couple of tourists into a stupor, you couldn't arrange things any better. Ceremonies and endless folk dances and tea parties and Brownies with bouquets. Spare me. At least the Queen Mother got to go up the CN Tower and have a glass of gin last time she was here. But she had to insist.

My suggestion was that Charles and Di be given a taste of real life. Send them somewhere bizarre, like Eckville, Alberta, centre of the Zionist conspiracy theory. That'd cheer them right up.

Photo: Trish Wilde

Fiona's portrait, end of summer, 1983.

She Gets By

Every girl in Canada would like to be
   just like her,
And every boy is dying for the chance
   to catch her eye,
She's the prettiest princess yet,
She gets hot, but she don't sweat,
She's the fairest of the fair, Lady Di.

CHORUS:
Lady Di, Lady Di,
She's got no job but she gets by,
Hooked herself a decent guy
And he's high on Lady Di,
Lady D., Lady D.,
Traded off her privacy
for the light of celebrity,
Now she smiles for you and me,
Who knows why? – Lady Di.

People come from miles around
   to see what she is wearing,
All the local look-alikes are posing
   left and right,
Why is it that guys who look like Charles
   are not appearing?
Maybe they're around,
   but the photographers won't bite.

CHORUS:
Lady Di and what's his name get shown
   the sweetest places,
All the potholes have been filled,
   there's joy in every crowd,
But I'm sure they'd like the chance
   to really get to know us,
See the special places that make
   Canada so proud.

Send Diana to Eckville,
   she'd be welcome there,
She looks so Protestant, she could
   even have lunch with the mayor.
     (and Mr. Keegstra's *very* fussy)

Lady Di, Lady Di,
She's got no job, but she gets by,
Hooked herself a decent guy,
He's getting on, but he's still spry –
Lady D., Lady D.,
She's so satisfactory.
All the premiers agree,
They all sigh – for Lady Di.

Here's a royal family song that's never been sung. I tried to jump on the sucky duet bandwagon with this one. Maybe I should have sent it to Julio Iglesias and Diana Ross, but I neglect this aspect of my career terribly.

Doug Wilde, who performs with me most often, refused to sing this song with me.

"Hey, I'm just the sideman," he protested.

And it was a shame, because he can do a twitty British accent quite well.

And now the objects of the duet, that (still) cute Prince Andrew and soft porn actress Koo Stark, are broken up. Indeed, Ms. Stark even married another guy. Ain't life hard for songwriters?

Nancy and Rick Whitelaw sing "Julio and Diana Go to Mariposa" in concert at Toronto Free Theatre, October 1985.

Andy and Koo's Duet

KOO: When I look into your eyes and
realize I've caught the prize,
   Oooooh, baby,
ANDY: I see your face in a magazine or
up there on the silver screen,
   Ooooo, baby,
KOO: Cause you're the one they talk about
ANDY: You're the one there's
shock about,
BOTH: Aren't we the lucky ones!
KOO: Am I making you blush?
ANDY: Hey, it's just my royal flush.
KOO: Oooooh, baby, baby, baby,
ANDY: Kooo, baby baby baby.

ANDY: You got something that I need,
my army buddies all agreed,
   Oooooh, baby,
KOO: If I'm the best you've ever had,
why can't I meet your mom and dad?
   Oooh, baby,
ANDY: It's not that they believe the hype,
But Mom's just not a social type,
Let's wait a little while,
KOO: Are you lying to me?
ANDY: That's a possibility,
KOO: Oooooo, baby, baby, baby,
ANDY: Koooo, baby, baby, baby.

KOO: We're the talk of the town, my dear,
At times I wish we could disappear,
ANDY: I know a place we could stay
for free, I can ask me old aunt
for the key.

KOO: I see a man in uniform, it makes
me feel all soft and warm,
   Ooooh, baby,
ANDY: And when you're in your
working clothes,
I feel the same way,
   I suppose,
   Ooooh, baby,
KOO: Makes no difference that
you're royal, I'd be just as sweet
and loyal
If you had not a dime,
ANDY: Are you lying to me?
KOO: That's a possibility.
ANDY: Koooo, baby, baby, baby,
KOO: Oooooo, baby, baby, baby,
ANDY: Koooooo, baby, baby, baby,
KOO: Oooo, baby, baby, baby.

"Thirty Years a Princess," while scarcely a mainstream hit, did get my name into *People* magazine.

I'm going to tell this story because we should all know how the media works so that we can suspend our belief a bit when reading, well, almost anything.

I wrote "Thirty Years" when it was announced Lady Di was going to have a second baby. I thought, good news for her. But what about all those royal relatives who are in line for the throne? Every time Diana produces, they all move down a notch. I especially felt for Princess Anne, who seemed to be living in Diana's shadow anyway.

"Thirty Years" was included on my cassette, *The Sunday Morning Tapes*. I sent it around to CBC stations, but not to commercial radio programs.

Meanwhile, Judy Small, a wonderful Australian singer-songwriter, called and asked for permission to put "Thirty Years" on her new album.

I was greatly honoured by this, and issued a little press release.

One person to whom I sent this was Hal Davis, a friend who works on the *New York Post*. (Hey, we all have to eat!)

Hal will do anything he thinks will help my career. So he talked to the gossip columnist at the *Post* and soon an item appeared, tied in with a rumoured feud between princesses Anne and Diana. This item quoted a line from my song, and said it was receiving "major airplay" in "several Commonwealth countries, including Canada and Australia"!!

I don't think even CBC Toronto had played the song, except for its original performance on "Sunday Morning." And Judy Small's version wasn't even recorded at that point.

As a result of this item we got phone calls from "Entertainment Tonight" and *People*. "Entertainment Tonight" took a pass on it, although their correspondent in Toronto did an item for CITY TV here. But *People* ran a big chunk of the song, set in dark type in a box.

Then I sent the tape to the "Dr. Demento" radio show, which is syndicated all over the place, and they played it a couple of times.

So, that is my big commercial success. I hope you're all happy for me.

Here's the hit.

Thirty Years a Princess

Now don't you feel sorry for
   poor Princess Anne?
She seems so sincere, and she stands
   by her man!
But as each year goes by, through
   no fault of her own,
She moves another notch away
   from the throne.

Now Mark said to Annie on a
   grim winter's day,
"I hear that Dianey is in a family way."
Anne bravely smiled and she said
   "how very chic!"
But a little royal tear slid down
   the royal cheek.

'Cause she can ride, she can curtsey,
And she's got a long dress,
She can cut a mean ribbon,
And she can cut up the press,
But it's all been for nothing,
And it seems kind of mean,
To be thirty years a princess
And never a queen.

How must she be feeling,
   our poor Princess Anne?
She's been training for glory since
   her life began.
Well, it's true, in the saddle she's
   a regular champ,
But she's never gonna see her pretty face
   on a stamp.

But she can ride, she can curtsey,
And she's quite well-to-do,
She can stand up for hours
Without going to the loo,
But from her place on the short list
She watched fate intervene,
Now it's thirty years a princess
And never a queen.
Why did Charles go and marry
That baby machine?
Thirty years a princess
And never a queen.

Finally, a clutch of songs on the only native-born royal we Canadians have ever had.

Pierre Trudeau. No, I've never met him. In fact, I figure I'm the only woman singer in the country he's never dated.

But once I was at an Air Canada counter in Toronto and looked around and there HE was at the next counter, buying his own ticket to Ottawa. No bodyguards, no entourage. Just one young woman; I think she was from his staff.

She read a fashion magazine all the way to Ottawa; he ordered a glass of milk and looked like he was deep in thought. He was on the aisle, she in the middle, and I was in the window seat.

Hardly anyone bothered him. A few stolen glances, perhaps a couple of handshakes. Certainly I didn't have the nerve to talk to him. I mean, what do you say?

That was in October of 1979, and the next day he announced he was resigning as prime minister.

Who could blame him? Would you want to be leader of a country where you had to fly economy and buy your own ticket? Not me!

I wrote songs for "Sunday Morning" steadily from November 1976 to April 1979, so I churned out a lot of stuff about Pierre Elliott Trudeau. It was almost easy, because he was unique. His arrogance, his insouciance, his elegance, his wacky wife, kids born on Christmas day – lots of material was there.

At that time I was writing short songs, specific to events of the day. I didn't write a full-length Trudeau song until long after I'd left "Sunday Morning." The first was in June 1982. By this time Trudeau had been with us too long, and we had the impression that, although a flashing star on the international scene, he was sick to death of domestic politics. Oh, sir, excuse us for being ordinary, I said.

Pierre, Pierre, We're Sorry

Oh he's wonderful in England,
He's merveilleux in France,
He's poetry in motion
When they all get up to dance,
He makes us feel so proud
When he's off in Germany,
But he doesn't give a damn about
Canadians like you and me.

Pierre, Pierre, we're sorry we're so boring,
We lack the social graces and
    the continental touch,
Our cry for jobs is tedious,
    our problems are a bore,
And you're right, we protest too much.
        (We've got no backbone.)

He's articulate in Spanish,
He's a riot in Chinese,
He tosses off one-liners
With such apparent ease,
In European cities
He's a charmer without flaw,
There must be something funny
In the air of Ottawa.

Pierre, Pierre, we're sorry we're
    such whiners
We hate to bring you crashing back
    to cold reality,
Who cares about the Crow's Nest rates
When you're hobnobbing with the greats,
Forget that – go off and ski.
        (Like, ski off, eh?)

Oh he's highly educated,
Seems to be nobody's fool,
And, god, is he spectacular
In the swimming pool!
A prime minister who seems to know
What tennis shoes are for –
Too bad there's not a trampoline
On the House of Commons floor.

Pierre, Pierre, we're sorry we're
    so graceless,
If you shopped with us at K-Mart,
    well I'm sure you'd wear a frown,
You set such a fine example,
    but it seems we never learn,
Why not teach us a lesson and step down?
        (We don't deserve you!)
Teach us a lesson and step down!
        (We're so unworthy!)
Teach us a lesson and step down!
        (It would be hard on us, sir, but it
            would be for our own good.)

When I started writing again for "Sunday Morning" (spring of '83) the Tory leadership campaign was on, but Trudeau was back in the saddle as prime minister. (I missed Joe Clark's short Tory government. Whew!)

   Mr. T. was, as usual, playing games with the press about his expected resignation. It went on for months.

Maybe-not Waltz

Will he, won't he – make up his mind,
  could it
Be they – asked him – and he declined,
  it's a
Tom cat's game, and we're the mouse,
  and we're
Trapped with him, he's king of the House,
And he stuns us again with his charm and
  his faults
As we join in his maybe, maybe-not waltz.

Now Silver John Turner is biting his nails,
  and the
Pundits are all reading entrails,
There's a tearoom in Hull where the
  business is brisk, but the
Betmakers say, "betting's closed,
  too much risk,"
Is he indecisive or just being coy,
  love to dance with our maybe,
  maybe-not boy.

Fifteen long years we've been locked in
  this dance,
We long to change partners but miss
  every chance,
Help, it's Old Blue Eyes, he's trying to
  cut in, wants to
Save us from the new boy who leads
  with his chin.

So it's one two three, un deux trois,
  on with the dance, he says
"I can't leave now, got to give
  peace a chance, and my
Kids are in a decent school, and they'll
Stay there till Justin is ready to rule, and as
Regent, I'll go down as one of the greats,
  and I'm
Ready to serve if the Pope abdicates.

This was taken for the cover of the Globe and Mail's *TV guide when Nancy was doing "Sunday Morning" the first time around.*

Then, in the spring of 1984, Pierre Trudeau did resign. And many of us found that we kind of missed the guy, brat though he was.

This song is a Canadian version of that old country classic, "I'm So Lonesome Since you Left Me, It's Almost like Having You Here." Hope y'all enjoy it now.

As for the little phrases in the chorus, they're some of Trudeau's most famous comments to the Canadian people. Eventually he got tired of being so articulate, and just gave us the finger.

Your Sweet Words

I wanted you to go away
And let me be free
For a new life with somebody new,
It was no good, I bored you,
And you let me know it,
And everyone knew we were through,
Now you're going, my heart is breaking,
It's caught in the crunch,
And I've met some new guys
But they're such a dull bunch,
I remember our good times
And how well you ski,
And the sweet things you used to say to me.

"Where's Biafra?," "Just watch me!",
    "Why should I sell your wheat?"
And "honey, you know what you can eat!"

You were always such a flashy guy,
Our friends always wondered
What was it that you saw in me,
We were such a strange couple,
You were rich, I was jobless,
And I knew it was not meant to be;
There were times I was lonely,
You were cold and remote,
Still I'll bid you goodbye
With a lump in my throat,
They called you "philosopher king"
    through the years,
And your fine words still ring in my ears.

"Where's Biafra?," "Just watch me!",
    "Why should I sell your wheat?"
And "honey, you know what you can eat!"

(You were wonderful in England,
You were merveilleux in France,
You were poetry in motion when
they all got up to dance,
You're articulate in Spanish,
a riot in Chinese,
You tossed off those one-liners with
such apparent ease,[1]
Why, sweetheart, there are those
who say you've lots of faults
But I'll always love a man
who can do triple somersaults.)

"Where's Biafra?," "Just watch me!"
"Why should I sell your wheat?"
And "honey, you know what you can eat!"
Adieu, Pierre, adieu.

1. If these lines seem strangely familiar, it's 'cause
they're a direct lift from "Pierre, Pierre, We're
Sorry." I had long since stopped singing it, so it
seemed okay to recite them over the instrumental
bridge.

And for My Last Number . . .

If I were doing a concert I would never end with a tender, nostalgic ballad like "Your Sweet Words," so it seemed a not quite proper way to end a book either.

So I'd like to leave you with a quasi-poem about our home and native land. I wrote this to recite as an introduction to Murray McLaughlan's "Out Past the Timberline," a wonderful, loving song I sometimes do as an antidote to what's gone before.

I need it. Once when I was singing at Bobbins (now defunct) wine bar in Toronto, a customer yelled out, "Hey, Nancy, isn't there anything you like???"

I was crushed. I like so many things – raindrops on roses, whiskers on kittens – all that. I've put some of those things into this sincere hymn of praise to the uniqueness of Canada.

(Musical note: If you recite this, try to get a piano player such as Michael Creber of Vancouver to underscore it with "Land of the Silver Birch." I swear, there won't be a dry Canadian eye in the place.)

Canada Is

CANADA IS – the cry of the loon
   the click of ice skates on the
     backyard rink
   the swoosh of the falling dollar
CANADA IS – Gretzky worship
   it is – rye and ginger in a paper cup,
     the ritual exchange of toe rubbers
      at an urban party
CANADA IS – not voting for the candidate
   you like best
   it is – giving the press to Rough Trade but
     letting Tommy Hunter host the only
     national TV variety show
   it is – the demoralizing discovery that
     your passport is worth more
      than you are

CANADA IS – our very own graffiti:
   Is Barbara Amiel?
   it is – hot dogs in packages of eight,
     rolls in packages of six
   it is – the sweet summer scent of Muskol
     ("It's banned in the States, eh?
     Here, let me rub some on ya.")
CANADA IS – a handsome gift of
   jumper cables for Christmas
CANADA IS – being thrilled to get
   jumper cables for Christmas
     And best of all,
CANADA IS – CBC radio. That's what
   I miss most when I'm away.

Selected Melody Lines

Yuppie Love

Mrs. Linda

What Should I Wear to the Revolution?

Be My Love or Else

Thirty Years a Princess

Blessed Michael Hear Our Hymn of Joy

Your Sweet Words

No Farleys

I'm Glad that I Don't

French from France

Tiny Embryos

My FIRA's Gone

Yuppie Love

1. IF YOU SANDBLAST MY HOUSE   I'LL WAX YOUR B. M. W. ......

IF YOU SANDBLAST MY HOUSE   I'LL EVEN BROIL A FISH FOR YOU

AND JANIS AND JIMI   WILL SMILE DOWN FROM A-BOVE

AS WE FALL   IN YUPPIE   LOVE   2. I'M GONNA

LIFE   YUPPIE   LOVE   IT AIN'T NO   DIFFERENT   JUST A

LITTLE MORE   SECURE   I   CAN   WORK ON OUR   RE-

LA-TIONSHIP   WHILE I   GET A MAN I CURE   AND THOUGH OUR

YUPPIE   LOVE IS   DEEP AND STRONG I FEEL   COM--PLETELY   FREE

E7 ... B7

IT'S   EASIER   TO   GET A-WAY   FROM A

B7   E7   E7   D.S. AL ⊕

TWO CAR   FA...MI...LY   3. AND I WILL HAVE OUR

E7   E7   E7

WHY, I'M SO FIT, I COULD PROBABLY JOG THE 1500 MILES TO MY MOTHER'S HOUSE!

MULTINAN INC.

Mrs. Linda

What Should I Wear to the Revolution?

LA - LA-LA LA-LA-LA-LA- LA - LA LA LA LA LA
LA LA LA LA LA LA LA- WHAT SHOULD I WEAR TO THE REV-O-
LU - TION? IS IT DECLASS-- É TO DRESS LIKE CHÉ?
WHAT SHOULD I WEAR TO THE REVO------LUTION? SHOULD I WEAR
SOCKS WITH MY BIRKEN------STOCKS? NOW CORDUROY I
FIND IT ALWAYS TENDS TO WEAR SO THIN AND OLIVE GREEN QUITE FRANKLY DOESN'T
DO MUCH FOR MY SKIN WHAT SHOULD I WEAR TO THE REVO-----LUTION?
HEY CHAIRMAN MAO WHAT'S YOUR SO----LU-TION? D.C.

MULTINAN INC.
(CAPAC)

Be My Love or Else

2. THEY LIKED TO WALK A... ROUND THE GROUNDS ON A SUNDAY AFTERNOON

AND THEY TRADED MEDICATION WHEN THERE WAS A FULLISH MOON AND SHE

SAID, "I DON'T WANT CHILDREN MUCH", HE SAID "I THINK I KNOW BUT

I'VE A MIND TO HAVE A SON AND I'M CALLING HIM RAM...BO" SO

JOHN AND LESLIE A MATCH THAT'S MADE IN HEAVEN JOHN AND LESLIE THERE'S

SO MUCH THAT THEY SHARE NOW SHE HAS SOMETHING HE AIN'T GOT SHE'S A SOME-WHAT

BETTER SHOT BUT A PSYCHOPATH IN LOVE HE MAY NOT CARE HE JUST SAYS

"I'M SO GLAD YOU FINALLY FOUND ME WRAP YOUR LOVING ARM AROUND ME

JODIE COULDN'T TOUCH YOU IF SHE TRIED BE MY LOVE

HAVE MY BABY BE MY BRIDE"

Thirty Years a Princess

1. NOW

DON'T YOU FEEL SORRY FOR POOR PRINCESS ANNE? SHE

SEEMS SO SIN-CERE AND SHE STANDS BY HER MAN BUT AS

EACH YEAR GOES BY THROUGH NO FAULT OF HER OWN SHE MOVES A-

NO.......ther NOTCH A...WAY FROM THE THRONE NOW

TEAR ROLLED DOWN THE ROYAL CHEEK 'CUZ SHE CAN RIDE SHE CAN

CURTSEY AND SHE'S GOT A LONG DRESS SHE CAN CUT A MEAN

RIBBON SHE CAN CUT UP THE PRESS BUT IT'S

ALL BEEN FOR NOTHING AND IT SEEMS KIND OF ME............

.................EAN TO BE THIRTY YEARS A

PRINCESS AND NEVER A QUEEN.

QUEEN WHY DID CHARLES GO AND MARRY THAT BABY MA —

CHI..................NE

THIRTY YEARS A PRINCESS AND NEVER A QUEEN

rit.... fine

MULTIMAN INC. (CAPAC)

Blessed Michael
Hear Our Hymn of Joy

1. BLESSED MICHAEL HEAR OUR HYMN OF JOY
WE BE-LIEVE YOU ARE THE HO-LY BOY YOU MUST BE GOD BE-CAUSE YOU
SING SO GOOD THY KINGDOM COME TO-DAY IN HOLLY -- WOOD
EV-ERY COMMAND WE O-----BEY FROM YOU YOU SAY TO "BEAT IT!" SO
REST ASSURED WE DO THE LIGHT BENEATH YOUR FOOTSTEPS IS A BEA-CON BRIGHT WE'LL
FOLLOW YOU LIKE CHILDREN 'THRU THE THRILLER NIGHT

DE CAPO AL CODA

4. OUT HERE IN AL BERTA WE'RE A
LONELY CREW WE MUST MEET IN SECRET JUST TO WOR -- SHIP YOU

HEATHEN PEOPLE HERE SAY YOU'RE NO DE - I - TY PLEASE FORGIVE THEM THEY BELIEVE IN

WAYNE GRETZKY A ···· MEN A ···· MEN A ·· A ·· A ·· A ···· MEN

MULTINAN INC. CAPAC

Your Sweet Words

Bb   A7   Dm   G   (SPOKEN)
- AFRA?   JUST   WATCH ME!   WHY SHOULD I SELL   YOUR   WHEAT?   AND

Gm   Am   Bb   Bb/c   C
HONEY   YOU   KNOW   WHAT   YOU   CAN   EAT

F   Bb   A7   Dm   D.C.
                                                          2x's
- SAULTS   WHERE'S   BI - AFRA?   JUST   WATCH ME!   WHY SHOULD I SELL   YOUR

G   Gm   Am   Bb
WHEAT?   AND   HONEY   YOU   KNOW   WHAT   YOU   C AN

Bb/c   F   Bb   A7
EAT   WHERE'S   BI - AFRA?   JUST   WATCH ME!   WHY SHOULD

Dm   G   Gm
I   SELL   YOUR   WHEAT?   AND   HONEY   YOU

Am   Bb   Gm/E   F
KNOW   WHAT   YOU   CAN   EAT   ADIEU PIERRE ADIEU

MULTINAN INC. (CAPAC)

127

No Farleys

1. WELL THE GREATEST COUNTRY IN THE WORLD IS THE GOOD OLE U.S.....A. AND EV---ERY BO.....DY IN THE WORLD BETTER DO WHAT THE U.S. SAY WE AIN'T SCARED OF ANY.....ONE THE RUSSIANS OR CHI....NESE BUT THERE'S A CERTAIN GUY WHO BRINGS US TREMBLING TO OUR KNEES! SO WE DON'T ALLOW NO FARLEYS A - ROUND HERE NO! WE DON'T ALLOW NO FARLEYS A - ROUND HERE 2. WE HERE NO FARLEYS WE'RE SORRY WE'RE

NOT GOING TO BACK DOWN NO PINKOS NO WEIRDOS IT'S

TIME FOR A CRACK DOWN WE DON'T NEED OUR FILES TO ES-

TA-BLISH HIS GUILT AND WHO CAN SAY WHAT HE KEEPS

(SPOKEN)

UNDER HIS KILT OOH! IS THAT A BABY BELUGA? D.S. al CODA

THROW US A MOON (HOWL) SO WE DON'T ALLOW NO FARLEYS AROUND

HERE NO! WE DON'T ALLOW NO FARLEYS NO

COMMIE LOVIN' CHARLIES WE DON'T ALLOW NO FARLEYS AROUND

HERE. fine

MULTINAN INC. (CAPAC)

129

I'm Glad that I Don't

1. WHEN WINTER DIES AND SPRING HAS SPRUNG MY BLOOD BOILS UP AND I FEEL QUITE YOUNG. I ALMOST WANT TO GO OUTSIDE SO I ASK THE MAID TO OPEN THE WINDOWS WIDE · · · · · · · · · · · · I CALL FOR MY CAR AND I GO DOWNTOWN I BUY A HAT I BUY A GOWN AND though MY LIFE Can BE A BORE I'M GLAD THAT I DON'T WORK AT TIMOTHY'S STORE (SHE'S GLAD THAT SHE DON'T WORK AT TIMOTHY'S STORE)

2. OH THE STORE

WHEN IT'S

WINTER IN THE CITY AND THE STREETS ARE GREY + SHITTY I'M

GLAD THAT I DON'T HAVE TO GO ON STRIKE FOR YOUR

FEET HURT WHEN YOU PICKET AND I'D GET TOO COLD TOO STICK IT AND

WALKING UN-ES-CORTED ISN'T VERY LADY---- LIKE

WORK I'M GLAD THAT I DON'T WORK I'M GLAD THAT I DON'T

WORK AT Timothy's STORE. I'M ONE BIG SPENDER MY CITY MY CENTRE I'M

ONE BIG SPENDER MY CITY MY CENTRE ....

MULTINAN INC. (CAPAC)

French From France

1. WHEN WE SET OFF THOSE BOMBS IN MURU-RO - - - A NOBODY'S S'POSED TO MIND (SPOKEN) WE'RE SURPRISED THE GREEN - - - PEACE

CUCKOO BOYS ARE TREATING US SO UN - - - - - - KIND

FOR THE FOLKS WHO LIVE A - - - - - LONG THE SEINE

HEAR A LITTLE BOOM! AND THEY SAY "A - - - MEN" THEY FAVOUR THE

NEUTRON DANCE AS LONG AS IT'S NOT IN FRANCE

2. WE'RE THE FRENCH FROM FRANCE AND WE BLOW UP THE SEAS

OOH LA LA LA C'EST SI BOMB! WE'RE THE FRENCH FROM FRANCE AND WE

DO AS WE PLEASE OOH LA LA LA C'EST SI BOMB!

(SPOKEN) WHEN THE YANKEES GO TESTING WE SAY IT'S DE-PLORABLE BUT

WE DO THE SAME PEOPLE SAY "HOW ADORABLE WE CAN'T HELP OUR BE-

LIGERENT STANCE WE'RE THE FRENCH FROM FRANCE D. C. AL⊕

FRANCE BOOM! (fin)

MULTINAN INC.

Tiny Embryos

1. WE ARE FROZEN EMBRY-OS FROM DOWN AUSTRALIA WAY

ALL WE WANT'S A LITTLE WOMB WHERE WE COULD GROW AND PLAY

MOMMY'S DEAD AND DADDY DIDN'T LEAVE A CALLING CARD

WE'RE STILL IN A TEST TUBE AND AL---- READY LIFE IS HARD LIFE IS

HARD LIFE IS HARD WHEN YOU CAN'T GO OUT IN THE YARD LIFE IS

HARD LIFE IS HARD WHEN YOU CAN'T GO OUT IN THE YARD

fine

2. C / F / Em / Dm G7

YET SOME SAY THE WORLD IS FULL OF BABIES WHO DON'T HAVE E-

C / F / Em

NOUGH TO EAT HOME-LESS TI--NY ORPHANS WITH NO

D7 / G / F

SHOES U---PON THEIR TI--NY FEET SO THE A---TTENTION

E7 / Am / Gsus G / Dm

PAID TO US MAY SEEM A LITTLE FUNNY IF YOU THINK SO

Em / F / Gsus G / G G/B

YOU'RE FORGETTING WE COME FROM MO----NEY

D. S. AL FINE

MULTINAN INC. (CAPAC)

My FIRA's Gone

1. HELLO, BIG BOY. OH, HOW I'VE MISSED YOU! WON'T YOU COME

BACK TO ME WITH YOUR COWBOY CHARM! I ALWAYS LIKE A MAN WITH A LOT OF CASH

IN HIS JEANS I FEEL SO PROSPEROUS WHEN I HANG ON YOUR ARM

MIND I'M ON-LY SORRY I'VE NO BA-NA-NAS TO

GIVE YOU AND I CAN'T WORK CHEAP FOR YOU LIKE YOUR GIRL IN HONG KONG BUT I'LL BE

GOOD TO YOU AND YOU CAN ROUGH ME UP A BIT I KNOW YOU LIKE TO DO

THAT, MAKES YOU FEEL BIG AND STRO......NG SO LISTEN

HOT SHOT HEY WHEN YOU COMING O.....VER I CAN'T WAIT MUCH

F

C sus   C

LONGER   I GOT RENT TO   PAY   BABY ALL I

F   F7   Bb

HAVE IS YOURS   ALL I   ASK IS A   HELPING HAND   I WANNA BE

F/C   C   Bb   Am Gm   F

YOUR BEST FRIEND AND TAKE YOU ALL THE   WAY.

MULTINAN INC.

Discography

Nancy White's songs are available in three recorded collections, *The Sunday Morning Tapes, Nancy White – Unexpected,* and *What Should I Wear to the Revolution?*

The Sunday Morning Tapes, released October 1984. This is the best of Nancy's "Sunday Morning" material, upgraded in a commercial studio, packaged with liner notes and produced on real time high quality cassettes. Titles: Maybe -not Waltz, Your Sweet Words, Boystown-on-the-Rideau, T for Tactile, Are You Fit?, No Life at All, He Smiled on You, Life of Brian, Twenty Minute Sit-It-Out, Thirty Years a Princess, Mister Sincerity, Yuppie Love, Nancy and Ronnie in China, Kiss Our Tarmac. (Mouton C-4)

Nancy White – Unexpected, released October 1983. CBC financed the recording of this beautifully produced (Matt Zimbel, Bill Garrett) album. It has some humour in it, but more of it is romantic and thoughtful. Titles: When the Wino, Mrs. Linda, Florida Kitchenette, Snow Angel, Cocktail of Tears, Ballerina in the Wings, I Know Cuba (Like the Back of My Hand), Nous Sommes des Enfants, Every Dozen Years, Volver a los 17 – To Be 17 Again, Desaparecidos, Footprints on My Floor. (Mouton WRC1-3024) Available as LP or cassette.

What Should I Wear to the Revolution?, released January 1984. This cassette is a mixture – it includes a couple of "Sunday Morning" songs and a translation into English of a bittersweet song by Marcelo Puente, but mainly it's Nancy's serious political material. Like *The Sunday Morning Tapes* it's copied real time on quality cassettes. Titles: What Should I Wear to the Revolution?, La Maudite Guerre, Not a Game, Sterile Women Super Men, Scandal in Caracas, Children of War, Watch Over Liberty, Elliot Lake, She Gets By, My Friends from the Bar, Bullets and Guitars. (Mouton C-3)

Index of Songs

(All lyrics by Nancy White. Music by Nancy White except where noted. All songs published by Multinan Inc.) (CAPAC)

Lifestyle

Oh Those Tories

Delicious Stories

Religion

1. Born Again/67
2. Papal Bull/69
3. Kiss Our Tarmac/71
4. Blessed Michael Hear Our Hymn of Joy/76, 124 (music)

It's Outrageous

1. Mountie-in-the-Snow/78
    (Music D. Wilde)
2. We're the Banks/79
3. He Smiled on You/81
4. Don't Blame INCO/83
5. Happy Now?/85
6. Nancy and Ronnie in China/87
    (Music by N. White & D. Wilde)
7. Bats for Brats/89
8. T for Tactile/91
    (Music by N. White & D. Wilde)
9. Mr. Sincerity/92
10. No Farleys/93, 128 (music)
11. Big Shot Budget/94
12. French from France/97, 132 (music)
13. Dump It in the Third World/99

Royalty

And for My Last Number

Acknowledgements

First of all, thanks to the people at CBC Radio's "Sunday Morning" who have produced the songs or helped with ideas: Bob Carty, Robert Harris, Alan Guettel, Stuart McLean, Roger Bill, Norm Bolin, Margaret Daly, Doug Grant, Chris Thomas; to Trish Wilde who took many of the photographs for this book before she devastated me by moving to Calgary; to Rick Whitelaw for the charts and for great guitar playing in studio and on the road; to Greg Walsh for the muscles; to our various obliging technicians; to Robert Fulford whose review of the "Sunday Morning Tapes" suggested this book to the people at Methuen; to Tanya Long and her colleagues for much help and enthusiasm; to Laurence Siegel, my patient and creative manager; and most of all to Doug Wilde who turns my tunes into music and convinced me several years ago that people prefer this stuff to my sucky ballads.

Nancy White